[Binary]

L
0
G
1
c

Liminal Books is an imprint of Between the Lines Publishing. The Liminal Books name and logo are trademarks of Between the Lines Publishing.

Cover design by Suzanne Johnson

Between the Lines Publishing
1769 Lexington Avenue N, Ste 286
Roseville MN 55113
btwnthelines.com

Published November 2022

ISBN: (Paperback) 978-1-958901-07-6
ISBN: (Ebook) 978-1-958901-08-3

[Binary]

L
0
G
1
C

Tracy Ross

Table of Contents

--Unity can only be manifested by the Binary. Unity itself and the idea of Unity are already two…
                    Buddha.

--Logic is not a body of doctrine, but a mirror-image of the world. Logic is transcendental…
                    Ludwig Wittgenstein.

--The third quotient is metaphor behind the binary…
                    Anonymous.

Something's Killing the Messenger

What if I die here? What if I don't type fast enough? What if I get it wrong…?

Setting the scene, fade in, interior of bar where I met my father.

"I have been a promising writer for twenty years, dear…" he said to me at the end of the bar. "I am older than your father's deepest thought…"

"I know…" I said regrettably, giving the man a little knowing, whimsical smile.

I sighed and walked away, leaving him to stand there in an empty bar, twenty minutes before closing time, wondering why he came to this dump in the first place. He had been talking to strangers the entire night and it had become one of those outings that he had regretted, but desperately needed in his profession. You see, he had been writing all day, trying to catch the tiger

1

by the tail, and it had devoured him long ago, leaving a husk and some bones. The beast had ingested the meat of the flesh and left him a hollowed-out thing stuffed with written pages of his musings, the insides of his guts hanging out for all to see in full spectacle.

Each time he opened his mouth he put his foot in it. And it was hard to scrape the shit off his shoes, it was hard to let the words go, when half the time you were insulting people, and telling them that they were no talent hacks. I had been just a young thing, sincerely wanting to complement him and his writing and make a connection. I told him I was in a MFA program and asked him some ridiculous advice, something about revision and second drafts. He brushed it off, refused the compliment, spit it back at me, and said something sarcastic and nasty. He doesn't remember what, but it must have been damn effective, because I walked away like all the rest. It was then that he looked around and saw no one left to taunt or bounce insults off of in the room except the bartender and the mirror behind the bar, both of which he needed to keep the drinks and self-hate coming.

My father had run. He had left my expecting mother, the only person he loved, for Chicago, leaving her in the pastoral, quiet neighborhood of the Northern town, never to say a proper goodbye, only for her to wake up and notice him gone. The pangs of guilt had come shortly thereafter, seeping into his mind as he tried to finish the final draft of a science fiction trilogy for his publisher. The writing of science fiction kept things distanced, so much so that he could create other worlds in which he wasn't such a son of a bitch.

The young girl in the MFA program happened to be his daughter, who he did not know about, leaving my mother back in the rural towns of the North, to raise me to go looking for my estranged father, only to realize, he wasn't worth the plane ticket I had spent money on, and the truth of our lineage was mine to keep and carry. He wasn't worth it. He didn't deserve me. He didn't need to know he had a daughter. I was worth more than he had proved in the five minutes I sized him up and had decided then and there to leave my orphan baggage at his feet and never look back.

But this was my story. I was the survivor. The new breed of writers who would supersede the old guard with more truth and honesty than they could have ever mustered in the last half of the 20th century.

He would bring in aliens or dystopian wars and apocalyptic futures. He would never write on the page:

I AM A SON OF A BITCH...

That was another person's job--the rest of the world who he spit and threw shit at so that he could get them riled up enough to give him a bloody nose. Suicide by audience. Slow death by insults and disconnect. It was the writer's way to go.

So, being dismissed by my own father, I started walking along the theater district of Chicago and ended up at Graceland cemetery. It was a little past 4 am in the morning and the front gates were locked, so having my father's emaciated body by design, I wriggled through two slightly bent gate bars to the side of the cemetery, out of view of the nighttime traffic on Clark Street. I ended up along a red brick wall, following close to a small pond overlooking several expensive elaborate crypts and a large stone art nouveau fountain. I wandered over to a black iron bench and sat down in front of a statue of an angel holding a sword.

From my trench coat pocket, I took out one of my father's published paperbacks. It was his most famous and well received. I leafed through it with my thumb and finger, glancing again at all the notes in the margins I had fastidiously made in my reading, hoping to glean some inspiration for my own masterpiece. I had religiously dog-eared various pages in which I imagined I could one day, like my father, write the great American novel.

But it was then that I realized I was holding a torch for the wrong team.

My mother died of breast cancer a long time ago and she never got her due, not even from me.

I walked several steps forward and bent down at a small gravestone. It was a stranger's. I ran my fingers along the bas-relief stone. So much for the dead and forgotten. What is left beneath the touch, betrays what we forget. We reminisce with cold hands, trying to grasp at the straws of memory. Only to remember what the heart already knows. That we were cruel. That we overlooked. That we neglected. That we forsook those who we loved. Transparency's a bitch, especially if it is your own shadow. And what you thought once was, never really happened, you only perceived it did for your own benefit. Sentimental delusion.

"Sandy…" someone called behind me. I jumped up startled, my heart stopping momentarily as I turned around. There in the half-light was my father standing there, looking perplexed and slightly pained. "You thought I didn't know…?" he said.

I looked at the man who I had both loved and hated, and stood perfectly still, holding onto his paperback book, realizing that he had recognized me, knew who I was all along.

"You look just like your mother…" he said.

"Sorry, what do you want me to do about it…?" I sarcastically snorted, not knowing what to say.

There was a long silence. We looked at each other. I began to say something short and methodical…but awkward just the same.

"She died six years ago…" I said.

He looked down.

"From what…" he asked still looking down and drawing a line in the gravel with his left shoe.

"Cancer." I stated flatly. "She suffered…"

My father looked up and smiled half a smile.

"I can imagine…"

"No, you can't." I added abruptly.

We both looked down. He reached out his hand. I reached out mine but pulled it back. They almost touched mid-way, but didn't, both of them returning back to our sides.

"Come here." he said and waived a finger in my direction and then to his left. "Let us go over here, I want to show you something."

I saw the moon; it was half full. I thought of a glass of water. I saw it half empty. I closed my eyes and the thought disappeared. I followed my father as he went over to a small flowing pond to the side of the graves. It was just before sunrise, very late or very early in the morning, I couldn't tell which.

We stood silent at the edge of the pond.

"Give me the book…" he said, holding out his skinny hand, palm outward.

"No." I quickly said, curling my right-handed fingers around it tightly, clutching it like a Bible.

"Give me the book, Sandy…" he asked again, his hand still raised in midair, the moonlight catching the wrinkles in his palm.

I thought for a minute, I saw my mother gasping for breath the night she died, her death rattle of a moan filling the house with the noise of pain. I closed my eyes and let the thought go. I closed my eyes and stretched the book out. I felt it slip from my fingers. I opened my eyes and my father had taken it from me. I saw the profile of his face in the shadows, the silvery light drawing a perfect white strip from his forehead down to his chin, illuminating the line of his face in the darkness.

He arched his hand back holding the paperback and looked over at me, smiling.

"I'm sorry, Sandy…" he said and threw the book far and away into the pond. It made a splash noise and promptly disappeared.

We then said nothing, staring at the pond. It was silent. We were silent.

Then I said something, something unexpected but otherwise necessary. It had come out of me like a sigh, the exhaling of a breath that I had held in a long time. Both my father and I were looking at the pond, thinking.

"I'm sorry, Mom." I whispered out loud for the both of us. It was then that I looked over at my father. It was then that he reached a hand out and as it brushed against mine, I grabbed gently onto it in return.

The sun started to rise, and we crept back into the Chicago street through the broken fence. We started to walk and found the nearest greasy spoon. It was 5 am in the morning. I was treated to a cheese and mushroom omelet and strong coffee. We started to talk about writing. We started to heal.

Requiem

I had a mentor that I cared for very much. She got me writing poetry in the first place when I was all but the age of 10. Almost six decades later, in a hospital in Chicago on the seventh floor overlooking Lake Shore Drive, she tried to say her goodbyes as I sat by her bedside and waited. We started out friends in grammar school and by the age of 21 at Northwestern University, she had become very well known.

Sara had gotten rather heavily into Buddhism and Eastern thought and went through bouts of fasting and transcendental meditation, only to fall off the wagon into episodes of major self-doubt and total hedonism which usually lead to weekend blackouts where she drank herself stupid. Often, she could be belligerent despite her dabbling in Eastern philosophy and maintaining a self-effacing demeanor, which resulted in her having an ornery facade that rubbed most people the wrong way. She never could decide whether she was really a self-absorbed ass or just appeared like one to most people she met. Either way, the mask fused with the woman's insides. Either way, no one really liked her all that much and I was one of the last friends she managed to retain in her isolated, estranged life.

"Maxine!" she yelled from the hospital bed.

I jumped out of surprise and immediately shook off the tension, not realizing I was that nervous at this supposed subdued time of quiet reflection.

"I'm right here, Sara…" I answered, still sitting on the side of her bed.

"What would it take for a woman to get some red roses in here?" she asked quietly.

I was tired and sad. I didn't fully register what she had said, or what she was asking for.

"Red roses?" I mumbled back at her, half smiling.

"Yes, Maxine." she looked straight at me as if I were stupid, her impatient, familiar look of tolerance. "Would you get me some roses in here?"

After making a small gesture of putting an index finger to my lips as if momentarily lost in thought, I left her bedside for the hallway. I stood outside the room with my hands on my hips, looking down, and exhaled.

The hospital gift shop was closed this late at night, but I remembered a kiosk about a block down from the hospital that sold magazines and flowers. I took the elevator down and started for the door. It had started to drizzle and the yellow lights from the lamps illuminated the street in a sickly glow that I had become very familiar with during my time living in Chicago. The sidewalk had already turned slick with the rain coming down and I sped up my pace to avoid getting totally wet.

When I got to the kiosk, all I could find was a small bouquet of carnations with daisies mixed in and one red rose sticking awkwardly out of it for good measure. I bought it and rushed my way back. When I entered Sara's room, I found her lying there with one hand holding her head, the other grasping on to the food tray at her side. She was quietly crying. Her shoulders were shaking. When I came in, she looked up, her eyes red and tired. Then, with all the strength she could muster, she pushed the food tray, which was on wheels, halfway across the room. It rolled successfully then stopped about mid-way, leaving me to navigate around it to sit back down on the side of the bed with my gift of flowers.

"Here you go, friend." I said, holding them out until she took the bunch with one hand, wiping her cheek with the other.

We sat in silence as she turned the bouquet slowly around in her fingers, looking it over as if she had never seen anything so beautiful. I just sat there and smiled. I didn't say a word. She didn't say a word. It was wrapped in very thin green paper and the rose in the center had caught several rain drops on its petals from the outside.

She smiled a little smile to herself. Then her brow furrowed, and she looked up at me from the flowers. She looked up as if a thought had just occurred to her. Before she said the words, she let out a little laugh while looking into my eyes. I was confused.

Then she said the words which I will never forget.

"Maxine," she spoke softly, holding on to the flowers tighter. "I disgust myself."

We just looked at each other silently.

My lips parted slightly as if I was about to say something, but then again, I remained silent.

Sara looked down.

I grabbed onto her hands holding the bouquet with a solitary clasp. Then before I knew it, I was standing up. Her eyes followed me. We stared at each other. Suddenly, with a terrible fear in my heart, I started to back away. I continued feeling my way behind me to the door, held up a hand to wave a silent goodbye, and then left Sara for the last time.

I couldn't breathe. I ran through the hall to the elevator and made my way down. When the doors opened, I quickly ran out into the Chicago night and hailed a cab to the nearest bar. I found myself sitting on a stool in front of a long mirror. The bartender brought my drink and I slammed it down. I ordered another.

I saw myself in the reflection across the bar. I stared right into my face, and I swear I didn't recognize myself. I started thinking about Sara. She had gone to Tangiers to write about it. She had joined a Tibetan monastery for six months and wrote about it. She had flown halfway around the world and drew metaphors out of the sky. I was afraid. Her last words echoed in my ears. The look in her eyes frightened me to the core of my being. I thought about going back. I thought about running back in the rain and saying something to her, something reassuring, something probably idiotic but consoling.

Then, upon looking at myself and having the same thought that Sara had verbalized on her death bed, I thought better of it. I couldn't stay with her until the bitter end. I couldn't face her after what she had let escape her lips.

"I disgust myself." I heard her say behind my closed eyes, taking another gulp of whisky. I opened my eyes and felt the burning liquid warm my throat, my chest in the damp September air of the drafty bar. If I had any guts, I would have gone back. I would have stayed. But she had revealed something about herself that I couldn't take. My heart was falling, and something had broken inside of me with those words.

"I disgust myself."

I blinked and my mind flashed back to the bouquet of flowers, the rain drops on the petals, the green wax paper wrinkled by the hands of a dying woman.

Four hours later the sun was rising. Four hours later I woke up in my own bed with a terrible hang over.

Why do I do this to myself?

I picked up my cell phone and saw the internet threading headlines. The second screen I had swiped to was the internet blurb:

Famous Chicago Poet, Sara Davies, Dies at 72

Then below the headline I read the sentence:

The guru of a generation that inspired millions, dies surrounded by loved ones.

I threw the phone on the bed and wrapped my blanket around me.

I knew the truth.

There were no loved ones.

There was no guru.

There was no generation.

There had only been a woman begging for roses and I had only managed to bring her one.

I looked across the room to the apartment windows.

It was storming hard, and the sheets of rain obscured my vision.

All I could think of was how the rain does fall.

I tried to get ready for the day.

I tried to write despite the rain.

Nor Any Drop to Drink

"Pain may be said to follow pleasure as its
shadow; but the misfortune is that in this
particular case, the substance belongs to the
shadow, the emptiness to its cause."
— Charles Caleb Colton

My name is Joshua. I am afraid of people and to curb
the pangs of loneliness, I drink. Because my father had
been alcoholic, with unpredictable behavior, I had
learned early on not to trust appearances and had also
trained myself in the process to distrust the world. But
everyone has reasons on why they drink, mine is just
slightly different like all the rest. I am middle aged now,
without a partner, without children, without a family,
and I live my life day by day with the best hope I can
muster, usually drunk. I had always been told by those
who once had my best interests in mind, that I had an

16

addictive personality, and I should beware of my desires. But it wasn't the alcohol I was addicted to; it was my own company when I was drunk that sealed the deal. I couldn't stand to be by myself sober. So, the evening of my father's death, I toasted to him with a stiff drink and haven't stopped since. I took pride in carrying on the tradition and was a very dedicated drunk, so much so that I really had time for nothing else.

Then came the monsters, those little funny creatures who beg you to do the reckoning. They enter your life just when you think maybe you can get away with it without much suffering.

I had met the first of the shadows the morning after my father had died and I woke up with a hangover, only to pour myself another drink to get over the nausea and headache. One minute they were there. I took a drink. The next minute, they were gone. I quickly learned that alcohol worked by preventing oxygen from getting to your brain, so you quickly felt relaxed and numb. The monsters did not have bodies in the normal sense of the word. They only appeared to people who, like me, had a history of them in the family. They were, in effect, familiars, like cats to the Egyptian pharaohs, but to those who took to drinking. The monsters, being home to a suffering, dying planet, chose to teleport and cross over to our parallel universe for company and companionship for this is the only way they could survive, to preserve their existence in the minds of poor souls like me.

But today was different because I was to step away. I was to separate myself from the desire. I was tired of being alone and scared of the world. I missed the others, others like myself. Humans. Let me explain the method that led to my madness.

Alcohol, once it got into the veins through the stomach, and into the blood, hitting the brain, was better than anything I had every felt on my terrestrial plane. It made me feel as if, like Plato, I had attained the Divine truth, the separation of body and soul, without the benefit of actually being deceased and having the cache to come back and tell about it. I kept a journal, my *Drink Me* journal and wrote down a log of my submersions, so much so that in five years, I had filled two thousand pages. Yet, when I would go back to the page, sit down in my sober, Earthly realm, it didn't quite make sense. What did make sense was that I had isolated myself in my life so much so, between the alcohol and my *Drink Me* journal, that I was utterly, totally alone.

But the jig was up when I started getting stomach cramps. I had hoped the shadows would bring me some phantasmagorical companionship, some semblance of peace, but the situation had been unresolved and yielded only yearning. I had not been in control of summoning them. They came after the stomach cramps when I didn't drink for a while. And after five years of hard drinking, they appeared to me in the most acute periods of withdrawal.

But the monsters made it personal. They had invaded my personal space. The phantoms would manifest out of the shadows and corners of rooms, making their ways to chairs and table tops and sit there, sometimes dancing, sometimes performing the mimicry of small shadowy whirlwinds that slowly rotated in place like perfectly manifesting nebulae . In the years that I had been drinking and attempting to get sober to the point of cramps, I had captured dozens of tiny nebulae in a variety of jars and containers within my apartment from the shadowy corners of my room, stored against the far side of the wall of the living room. They remained there, within their containers, some see through, others not, churning inside the jars, tiny, small faces morphing and making painful faces at me. Never sleeping, never dying, never disappearing, to be with me in my apartment forever.

But I was smart, or so I thought. I had concluded that the little shadowy faces were a physical form of DTs produced from the withdrawal of the alcohol. They only came out when the stomach cramps came, leaving me to pick up a scotch on the rocks in defense. It was then that, after catching a smokey shadow within a jar and sealing it shut, that I realized, something, some force had helped to manifest the little clouds of pain into real, alive three-dimensional things to be reckoned with by any means necessary.

On the morning the 10th year of my father's premature death, I had had enough. After several days without a drink, I could endure the withdrawal no longer and again, I fell to my apartment floor in panic, sweating and shaking. After about six rounds of the cramps, a monster started transforming through the wall, swirling around as the familiar dark shadow I knew so well. I just stared at it, tears rolling down my face. I scrambled to a newly bought case of mason jars that I had mail ordered from a cooking supply outfit and grabbed one of the glass containers.

With swift dexterity and finesse, I caught the cloud creature from midair into the jar and closed the lid fast. It was then that the tiny shadow turned into an obscure human likeness and faced me in captivity. It was then that I had made up my mind to confront the situation.

With all the courage I could muster, I finally had a question for the many faces. A question that they would have to answer.

"Hey Jack," I said to the perfectly proportioned little screaming face, five inches tall, silent mouth gaping and eyes winced in turmoil, waiting for me to cave in and reach for a drink. "What the hell is all this then…! Do you expect me to collect my DTs in mason jars for the rest of my life? What is this nonsense...?

Rewind back to my father. I was starting to understand. You see, my father had passed down to me his little friends. They had kept him company, but ultimately, like my situation, they had made him miserable. It would have to be either me or them, the manifested shadows of addiction, who would break through to the other side and survive this legacy of suffering. To keep the monsters at bay, I would have to refrain from reaching for another drink, to stop the cycle, to stop the hunger once and for all.

And this is what I did. Somewhere in the anguish of the night, floating in the double glass doors of my high-rise balcony, I was visited by a shadowy apparition of my father. I even felt the cold of the night come in as he passed through the entryway, walked toward me in his suit and tie, and bent down, kneeling before me as I clung to a blanket in the corner of the room. He was in his prime, maybe in his forties, at the height of his career, with salt and pepper hair and silver cuff links fastening white sleeves around thin wrists.

I felt like I was dying. He had come to comfort me in my pain.

"Joshua," he questioned. "Joshua…" he repeated and reached out a hand and stroked the side of my face. "I know you don't understand right now." he explained, "but you will in time. Don't mind the pink elephants…"

And with that he was gone. Into the shadows from whence he came.

It was then that I realized I was in it for the both of us. My father and I against the anguish. At one point, during the early hours of morning, the crying faces had all gotten loose and were crawling up the walls and dropping from the ceiling like smokey apparitions from Dante's Inferno, liquid shadows of creeping hunger, an infestation of screaming mouths and terror-stricken eyes, the reality of the walls closing in on me like a wriggling, dark prison. In my panic and shock, I finally blacked out, leaving the room for the numbing promise of sleep. I welcomed unconscious bliss.

Note to self: pain is a manifestation. It lives like a beast, a breathing, hungry creature, unable to free itself from destiny, unable to make the choice to release itself because it is comfortable in its tragedy. It is easier to go on in pain, then to go through to the other side where there is peace. The fear stops you. It prevents you from going all the way.

"Don't mind the pink elephants…"

When morning came and I uncurled from the floor in a puddle of sweaty clothes and sheets, what I saw was phenomenal.

Along the walls of my apartment were the mason jars, the containers I had collected. There were about a hundred of them and they were all now empty. But it was when I went to the mirror above the liquor cabinet and looked at myself smiling and said, "Don't mind the pink elephants…" that I realized the jars had always been empty. Sometimes it is the emptiness at the bottom of the glass that gives you everything. Sometimes the delusion is what it takes to show you that nothing is behind the pain once you step into the light.

Behind the Hollywood Sign

The smell of exhaust and gasoline. Cars speed by like fading holograms in the rain, transmissions interrupted, moving visual blobs in the sensory flux.

The madness is hidden beneath the new wave of automation, the technology masking the ancient face of a dark carnal ritual. Beneath the bustling feet and pavement resides the ancestral underworld who listen to the descendants above and catch the whispers of playing children—and the sons and daughters do indeed play and the machinery churns by itself in this brilliant new factory.

Hollywood—where the haunted Old-World spirits permeate the crumbling building walls and cast long black shadows on the modern glass and steel. There is laughter in the wind, there are souls lingering in the decaying brick and mortar, there are insomniac dreamers roaming in the town where the dead never sleep. This is the warm, enveloping cradle of my birth. This is where my young eager retinal nerves absorbed the tired images of the celluloid mother of the future.

Don't fear me. I'm as harmless as a saline solution, as weightless as air, as subtle as Sunday evening's twilight when the dark colors of blue and purple merge leaving the sky bruised.

Born naked and dreamless in America's black metal dumpster, the colorful debris became my quilt, and I awoke with yesterday's newspapers beneath my head. And because I was naked and had no home, I got arrested for indecent exposure and the police who hauled me off asked me the name of the president of the United States while putting me in hand cuffs. I told them the garbage kept me warm and I had just ventured into this new estranged world. They threw a blanket over my bare shoulders and drove me to the station. There they gave me some ill-fitting clothes and placed me in a cell where other men stood and waited.

I remember as a child in the dumpster I was a prodigy and could paint anything like Michelangelo. The lid of the metal garbage container became my Sistine Chapel and I tried with each brush stroke to paint the face of God among the rubble and discarded trash.

In my enclosed world I had everything imaginable to work with—free magazines, unwanted books, scratched CD's and DVD's, dysfunctional machinery and electronics, half consumed brightly colored food packages and unused cosmetics and medication. My birthplace was where the media machine waste trickled down and I remained in Limbo where there was a lag time between what happened on the outside world and what I finally digested from within my dumpster walls. Last year's entertainment became food for today's meal, and I ravenously read about celebrities and looked over faces that were already ghosts in the public eye. From within my decaying steel womb, I created my own working technology from the broken mechanical parts and stray wires all around me.

Suffering from the madness inherent in my very bones and closing in on my mind like the imprisoning space surrounding me, I self-medicated with the trash pharmacopoeia in my desperate reach. Grasping for a half-used tube there and half-full pill bottle here, a bit of gauze there and an expired box of vitamins here, I treated the flesh and blood leaving the brain to the incoming flow of media garbage.

Barefoot and homeless, I was led by the hand down the police station stairs. The limousine was waiting for me again. I got in the car, and we drove smoothly through the shadowy LA streets which glistened like black glass from an early evening rain. With the bullet proof windows tightly shut, we passed the locked-up store fronts, the leaning apartment buildings, the wandering nighthawks buying booze at all-night convenience stores, the closed churches and the 24-hour Quickie-Marts.

Being a confused witness to the city's endless panoramic collage, it was there in the merge of complete alienation, isolation, and confusion that I realized who I was. I was a creature of immortal endurance, a member of the quiet sad species beneath the mass-produced generation above ground. I now understood. The faces and names on the garbage fueled the great machine which pried currency from the warm eager hands of young babes wanting to live forever. What most didn't realize was that stars live a very long time.

The limousine stopped at an old, refurbished apartment building with modern windows, surrounded by a tall black iron fence. There was a barrier of security at each step. I stopped before the gate and punched in some numbers on a keypad, then I came up to the first front doorway and I did the same on a second keypad. The door buzzed and I then stood in a small hallway where my security let me through to a small corridor with an elevator. There one of the *suits* swiped a card through a magnetic strip and I punched in more numbers. The metal doors opened, closed, and I rode silently upward, where, after several seconds the door opened directly into a large loft.

I am the neon that cuts through the elusive noir of night like the buzzing lights of a thousand electrified blaring words advertising Hollywood. The transformation starts again. My blood and plasma quickly turn from nature's internal river into the eternal stream of brilliantly charged light. I become the hero of the late show during the lonely urban nocturnal hour, offering my salvation like a traveling carnival's magician rummaging through his cheap bag of tricks, searching for that one object of illusion to suspend your belief.

My light plays in the shadows and my hybrid presence seeps into every concrete crevice, into every hidden nook and narrow alley, into the instinctual vice of the dark city dweller's mind. My new blood bathes the architectural geometry of Hollywood in a glowing liquid aura that hangs off the roof tops and windowpanes like a surreal, pliable, plastic skin. The transformers. We are the building's gargoyles and dragons, angels and cherubs, our preserved faces glowing a pale crimson red and sickly yellow in the half-light from the electrified streets below. I am a star again. I am very tired.

So here I am. I try to wear the clothes. I try to cloak myself in the walk, in the talk, in the sane behavior of a man who knows what the fuck is going on. I try not to let my hybrid existence get in the way. I laugh at the punch lines without getting the joke. I thank the movie studio for giving me back wrong change. I button my collar up tight and straighten my tie, brushing off the Armani suit for battle.

Before the dog tag around my neck, before I was a face in the film can, there was a way to touch the waters of the shore, a way to redeem the heart even as a child in that world of garbage. But now I look for dreams in sleeping children. This is my home. If you taste my lips, I will betray everything you hold true with a kiss and leave, taking the desire, taking your muse. If you want my time, you must resign and pay the price, you must accept the consequence.

A woman was putting make-up on my face. I felt like I had been run over by a truck. The bones still weren't clicking into place. The flesh still wasn't settling in. My eyeballs were lazy in their sockets. There was a guy in sunglasses at my elbow. He drank repeatedly from a long water bottle. The director.

What was I selling this time? What did I want them to want?

That's when I fainted.

I could feel the inside dumpster walls surrounding me like a cocoon once again. But the cops were on to me for being naked in the trash for the second time this month and I was back again at the station waiting for my limousine. When it came, I was driven to a different place this time.

We were headed in the direction of the desert, and it didn't take us long to come upon the hill in the distance. The car stopped.

I saw, through my tinted bullet proof window the silhouette of a scarecrow against the rising sun stuck in the bare sand. The limo doors clicked unlocked. In my bare feet I got out wearing the robe the cops had given me. My chauffeur's mirrored window was up so I could not see who drove me. I wrapped the Terry cloth robe around tighter and tapped a knuckle against my own reflection in his window glass. The window slid down.

"Why is there a scarecrow in the middle of nowhere?" I asked.

"It's not a scarecrow."

"Why am I here?" I asked.

"You forget."

"Forget what?"

"Your line."

"What line!" I cried, exasperated, and tired.

"The heartbeat. Flat lining will never be an option for you…ever."

I then realized I had been in this situation may times before, resurrected from the tomb.

The chauffeur's window went up and I got back in the rear seat. As the car drove away, the sun rose and the crucified *scarecrow* disintegrated to dust, a white cloud of smoke ascending upward, and I was left in the wasteland forever. When we headed back into town, I finally saw the back of the Hollywood sign. In a red graffiti scrawl were written the three words, "God help me!" I pressed a button and the black partition between me and my driver disappeared. I looked down to the front seat where above I saw my driver's eyes in the mirror looking back at me as a small crucifix dangled from a chain. That's when I fainted yet again.

I smell garbage.

I am very tired.

The Pins

"And when I am formulated, sprawling on a
pin, when I am pinned and wriggling on the
wall, then how should I begin to spit out all
the butt-ends of my days and ways? And how
should I presume?"
---T. S. Eliot, The Love Song of J. Alfred
Prufrock,1920.

I will never forget the moment when little Howdy
Doody, a sixteen-year-old freckled faced boy from
Oregon, pinned my queen in the line of the attack of the
rook during the twenty fourth move. I literally had no
choice but to resign at that point. I can still hear the
plunger of the clock coming down with a final quick
stabbing motion and my realizing my horrible mistake.
My Elo rating had been in jeopardy up to game five in
the tournament and I now wasn't going to move forward.

At the ripe old age of seventeen my entire chess career was over. Howdy Doody, my younger adversary, stood up quickly, his wooden chair making a terrible screeching sound against the hard floor. He just victoriously pointed a finger at me after they tallied up his score and held his arm up as the applause spread through the auditorium.

If I had foresaw earlier down the line, if I hadn't traded knights in move fourteen, if I had concentrated more, if the back of my chair were straighter and my seat didn't squeak, then maybe things would have been different...

Later in my hotel room with my parents and my coach, the air was stifling with silent disappointment, and I sat on the edge of my single bed with my head in my hands in mortification of what I had not done--won the chess tournament. My family had invested time, money and sweat into my natural talent for the game, but it had never been my dream, it had always been someone else's. I hadn't even placed second or third, a rating worthy of my eleven years of playing, touring from one tournament to the next, state to state, city to city until I couldn't remember my own name let alone where I had started. Each move of my and Howdy Doody's game was now forever burnt into my brain, a dismal flight plan etched in stone, preserving for me a gruesome reference point of failure for the rest of my life. Painfully, brilliantly my winning opponent had used a "pin" strategy to give me no other choice but to forfeit pieces one by one and gradually relinquish my position on the board.

I sat in my small room back home and mulled repeatedly over each decision I had made with the pieces, fastidiously motioning my hands and fingers about over an imaginary board, my eyes closed in a trance as if I could turn back time to give me one more chance...Please, God...one more chance. Yet, that chance never came.

Twenty years older and none the wiser...

"What do you mean, I have no friends?" I asked in the back of the taxi.

"You just *said* you have no friends." Bill reminded me.

My hands had started to shake again. It had started to rain, and I lowered my eyes, the depression and tension settling in.

"Yes, but it means something insulting coming from you." I pointed out. "You have no right to imply I'm an asshole. Now me, I have every right. You don't know me...You never really knew me."

Bill cleared his throat.

"How can you say that," he accused. "I've known you for forty years. I've suffered with your neuroses my entire life. Mom even said so. I'm a saint, the best big brother you'll ever have. Yes. I have a right, asshole..."

I shook my hands from the wrists like Kermit the Frog at the beginning of the Muppet Show. My skin started to crawl. I shrugged my shoulders as if I were already in the rain. I could feel the cold. The winter was closing in.

"Why does mom have to settle everything for you even when she's not here?!" I yelled.

My brother pointed a finger and then waved his hand away.

"Because you're always wrong," he said, "that's why."

At that point we just sighed, turning our heads separately away toward the windows of the back seat.

"Tell the cab driver where you want to go, Alex."

"You tell him, you know where we're headed, too!" I added indignantly.

"In your usual fashion, you're Pontius Pilate again? Tell him where you want to go, Alex."

"No!"

Suddenly the car swerved to the side, pulled over at the curb and the driver stopped the taxi.

The cab driver didn't turn around but just yelled at the top of his lungs, the back of his blonde ponytail shaking back and forth behind bullet proof glass.

"All right, boys! Out of the car!" he demanded.

Both of us froze and turned away from each other to look out our prospective windows again, thinking we resolved the issue.

"Hey. Out!" the cabbie shouted. "I mean what I say, gentlemen. Out!"

Both of us suddenly scrambled for our door handles, quickly scampering out the taxi onto the street. The cab drove away, leaving us in the rain. I watched the cab as it disappeared. My frustration manifested itself in more twitching and shaking.

"Look what you did." I retorted.

"Look what *I* did?" Bill repeated.

"Don't use that condescending tone with me, buddy." I shouted. I was getting quietly hysterical again, a feeling I knew well and controlled with a habit of digging my nails into my palms. My whole body was in pain and my nerves felt like bundles of barbed wire rubbing on the inside of my skin.

"Hey, *fella*. This is why you don't have any friends." Bill pointed out. "You just don't get it, do you?! You're an obsessive compulsive, self-absorbed, germaphobe opiate freak who blames the world for your failures..."

"What!" I half asked and falsely defended myself in a high-pitched crackle. The exclamation was rhetorical and neither of us expected an answer. My infantile squeal just hung in the air damning me to further guilt about everything. I didn't know my brother suspected anything. I thought that after all these years I had at least kept the opiates under wraps.

What. The floodgates were open. The rain poured down in buckets. Suddenly my body went numb and there was an annoying hum in my ears. I stared at my brother through the rain.

I still had fucking metal pins in my back. The motorcycle accident was almost ten years ago, and I still had the fucking pins in my back. They would always be there like the stigmata of my ego, tearing into my brain. They would gnaw away between my shoulder blades for years and years until my last defiant breath swore obscenities, cursing the devil's biting teeth even in death.

A long pause and then a thick rush of blood pushed through my veins. Chicago traffic went on, people brushed by on the sidewalk in the afternoon rush, a siren in the distance howled and a car horn honked.

"If you only knew the kind of shit I have to deal with..." I croaked, wiping the water away from my forehead and up back through my hair.

"That's just it, Alex..." Bill looked down at the streaming water running into the gutter. "You don't *deal* with anything. You don't deal with always hurting people, sticking to the truth, or keeping your word. I'm talking about integrity of character, Alex--and you don't seem to have any. And don't give me that motorcycle accident shit that wasn't your fault either!"

At just that moment I lunged in the direction of my brother and took him down. We fell hard on the concrete. I heard my back crack. I also heard the familiar rattle in my left coat pocket. Bill knew what it was and went for it. Pills. Bill held me down fast and started rifling through my raincoat pockets.

"Ahh...Pink pastel ladies, right Alex!"

"Get off me!" I cried in a low guttural growl.

Bill had gotten a hold of them, then held them up in the air while keeping me squirming on my back. Then we thrashed about on the sidewalk some more, but the daily lunchtime crowds just walked by, oblivious to two nut-less monkeys rolling around in the rain.

"Scuse me, scuse me, scuse me..." People quickly scuttled by our bodies on the ground, caring more about lunchtime sustenance than stepping on some idiot's fat head. Scuse me, scuse me but you're fucking with my lunch break!

Bill had the pink pastel ladies over me alright.

"Is this what you want, Alex?" he shouted rattling the transparent brown pill bottle. "Is this all you care about!"

I froze and stopped my struggling. I knew I had

been defeated. I resigned again. I relaxed my tense muscles against the cold concrete.

"You son of a bitch!" Bill shouted and stopped, peeked upward and squinted at the bottle, the water running down the label.

"Yeah, Bill. You got me, brother!" I laughed triumphantly, half out of my mind with sadness.

Bill hurled the bottle in anger into the rain and it bounced off the forehead of a passerby with a leather jacket and Cubs baseball cap. Without skipping a beat, the stranger picked up the bottle between his feet, read the label and promptly shouted a "Thank you, man!" before shoving it into his jacket pocket and running off.

I started my cackling, a low-pitched scream that shook my whole body.

Bill looked down at me and smiled, then started to laugh too.

"Help me, will you." I finally motioned upward at my brother, my skinny frame and weak back unable to flip my own body back into an upright position.

Bill quickly stood up and looked down at my struggling on the wet concrete. I tried to prop myself up on my right elbow but kept slipping back down.

I looked sheepishly upward at my brother.

"The pins." I said sadly. "The pins..."

Bill let out a sigh of both resignation and

understanding.

"Yes...The pins... " Bill repeated. "The pins..."

Bill then offered his hand down to me. Silently, I took the hand and felt another hand cup the back of my left shoulder. The strength of my older brother's grip lifted me up to a dignified position, one in which I was eye level with the world again.

Then Bill winked at me, a drop of rain falling from his eye lash.

"Come with me, Alex?" Bill asked while straightening out my raincoat collar.

We walked for a while, down the street and then around the corner. He smiled faintly, the rain still coming down in sheets, a sensory flux of blurred traffic and bobbing heads tilting their umbrellas against the wind.

"Come on, Alex. Let's get out of this rain and I'll show you something."

I didn't know where we were going on foot, getting soaking wet, but I followed. I followed lagging behind like so many times before, using the back of my brother's shoes as a guide through the blinding streets, the blurred years.

Bill pointed down the street at the Field Museum of Natural History and we ran for it through the traffic and the crowds. I was confused but Bill bought two tickets for an exhibit down one of the long museum corridors. Before I knew it, we were alone in a pristine exhibition room. My eyes found it hard to adjust to the bright lights, by default being red and bloodshot.

So, there they were, hundreds of cases along the walls with hundreds of bugs of all shapes and sizes...beautiful insects of every color and species, organized from the smallest to the largest, from the rarest to the most common.

"I come here often," Bill confessed. He smiled again, a faint engineer's smile. He was always the practical one, so practical that he became an engineer for Boeing and outsourced the real people in his life.

"Watch and be amazed," he promised and took something black and square from his pocket. He ran the black square smoothly over one of the bug cases, gliding the magnet just over and above the glass but not touching it. Suddenly all the beetles fell to the bottom of the case. The pins had been somehow dislodged from the backs of the poor things, allowing them to fall. Bill looked at me and smiled. "Now, run!" We ran out of the museum back into the rain. I got out into the street doubled over and breathing hard. Bill was already hailing another taxi and getting into the car when he shouted back at me,

"Security in numbers, Alex!" he waved. "See you on

the flip side!"

It was then that I hailed my own taxi to rehab.

It was then that I realized I wasn't so alone, it was then that I let myself fall...pins and all...

American Headquarters

Thursday night. The eight-foot-tall plastic restaurant trademark was pressing its brightly colored face against my bedroom window again. He managed to attach himself to the building three flights up and flattened his bulging blue eyes and perpetually smiling red lips against the glass.

This was his fifth night visiting me and I finally decided to get the 32-caliber automatic out of the drawer. His tall, chubby body was made out of a type of plastic that could alternate from being very hard and stiff to very flesh-like and flexible. Each night, dressed in his clownish blue and white-checkered overalls and t-shirt, he hovered by the window, holding a hamburger up by a permanently raised hand, and flattened his face to see me. When I went forward from my bed to investigate, he would move away, instantly popping his pinkish face to hard, glistening features.

BIG JOE.

I've known him for years.

As a child, my brother and I were taken to the red-bricked restaurant every other Friday when our father got paid from the office. BIG JOE had many family diners in his successful franchise, but my favorite was about a mile from our house. Whenever the family car approached the diner my brother and I would become ecstatic at the sight of BIG JOE turning on his platform under tiny spotlights.

Through car windows, I would see BIG JOE turning in the surreal quiet of night with his cartoon-ish pink face, shining eyes and lacquered wave of blond hair beaming with optimistic commercialism. He smiled endlessly, trying to lure other late-night drivers in for a taste of grilled hamburger patties squished between doughy buns with re-warmed frozen French fries. "FOOD FOR SALE", it said in the middle of suburban nowhere. "BIG JOE FOR SALE". Watching the turning statue, I often wondered what our suburban nowhere meant to me, meant to my dreams, and hopes, my belief in making the world somehow real. But BIG JOE was part of the family. He was our buddy, our ever-present friendly pal.

Ten years later, BIG JOE was here again, at my window like a freakish carnival prop. I pressed my hand to the glass and the monster hovered in the air inches from my face, staring and smiling at me with those painted features. Although there were no lights in sight, his body and face glowed ghoulishly from below. I held my silver automatic up and waved it in my hand to show him that I meant business. I tapped the gun against the glass and pointed the barrel at him, imagining firing a bullet in his overfed gut. He wouldn't move. He just floated there like a fucking Macy's Thanksgiving Day float.

Finally, I turned around and put the gun down on the night table. For the rest of the night, I watched BIG JOE at my window until I fell asleep. When I awoke the next morning BIG JOE was gone from my window but not gone for good.

Suddenly, out of nowhere, there he was again.

Out of the corner of my eye, a checkered jumpsuit and shock of blond hair edged past a wall of my apartment. Getting my gun from the bedroom, I followed him and went down the hall toward the dining room.

Fuck. There he was again. His smiling face peered at me from inside the bathroom. His arm and the hamburger he held up jutted out from the edge of the open door. I darted sideways and held the gun close to my side. He quickly moved out of sight. I cautiously inched my way toward the bathroom. Like a panning camera, my head turned and discovered only a wall of white tile and an empty shower. He had disappeared. Where had he gone?

I went back to my bedroom window again and looked out. Glancing down at the street, I saw him waiting at the bus stop. Other people waiting seemed completely unaware of his huge clownish body. I quickly got dressed, put my gun in my belt and, grabbing my wallet, headed out the door.

BIG JOE had made his body flexible and was squeezing his rubbery figure through the bus door when I approached the bus stop. I ran and got on behind him. As I slid my crumpled dollar in, the bus driver gave me an apprehensive look that made me self-conscious of my uncombed hair and sweaty face. BIG JOE's tall bulging frame brushed against the bus ceiling and against the shoulders of sitting riders who were oblivious to his squishing plastic skin. As he walked to the five empty seats at the back, his synthetic legs moved onward, producing an odd squeaking sound similar to two balloons being rubbed together. When he sat down his lifted arm and hamburger pressed against the window creating a mesh of crumpled fake food and pink flesh.

I nervously sat in one of the side seats. Because his painted features were fixed in a happy expression, he gave me no apparent sign that he knew who I was. The bus rode on for about twenty minutes and although no one seemed to see BIG JOE, no one approached the back for a seat. Finally, he awkwardly got up and went for the door. I followed. He squeezed himself through the doors of the back exit and I stumbled onto the curb after him.

In a split second I knew where I was. The red brick building and the smell of French fries instantly told me I had gotten off in front of a BIG JOE restaurant. To my surprise, when I looked for BIG JOE himself, I found him in the adjoining parking lot, standing on the roof of a parked car trying to climb up on his rotating stand that was unoccupied. Pudgy franchised bastard. He awkwardly bent his plastic legs and, with his arm still outstretched with a hamburger, slid up the pole and hoisted himself up on the small round platform. Once he positioned himself, he froze and became the turning statue of all BIG JOE diners seen scattered along the flat city landscape.

I approached the towering trademark and looked up. He was hard shiny plastic now, not a flexible creature. He was ignoring me, but I knew the game wasn't over. I went into the restaurant and took a booth close to the window in case he decided to climb off his stand to coax me to follow. Thirty minutes later I was eating my hamburger and he hadn't moved, just around and around he went, ambivalent to my waiting.

An hour went by, then another. The waitress refilled my coffee cup, brought me another hamburger, some fries. I sat there with the stoicism of a monk. I could wait there forever. It started getting darker. More coffee. The sun began to set. Another plate of fries. Blackness was now beyond my window and BIG JOE was in the spotlight, the glowing star of the urban night.

Then, as if a bolt of electricity had jolted my nerves, I angrily jumped from my booth, paid my bill, and ran back out into the parking lot. Again, I stood and looked up at the American icon, my childhood genie of fun and unlimited fast-food adventure. Round and round he went, glistening in the night like a garish Halloween freak from hell. Round and round he went, ignoring me, pretending that I didn't exist, didn't know of his ulterior plan.

I began to scream, low screams from the depths of my stomach. Over and over, I screamed, stretching my arms out as if expecting something, anything to answer my desperate plea.

"You rotten lousy bastard!" I yelled at him waving my gun in the air. "Come down and fight like a man, you cowardly hunk of polyurethane and circus paint!"

I aimlessly shot bullets into the air.

He didn't budge, just smiled, offering his hamburger to passing cars.

"Fuck you!" I ferociously growled, putting my gun back in my belt. "FUCK YOU!"

Frantically, I fumbled for the wallet in my back pocket and opened it. Taking out a five, I crumpled it and forcefully threw it up at him. It bounced off a gleaming white tooth.

"This is for you, BIG JOE!" I fumed, taking out a single, balling it up and flinging it.

Again, I wildly dug through my wallet, my teeth clenching.

I crumpled up another bill and paused, holding my arm back.

"This is for six years in college…for me being unemployed, overqualified, under-qualified, subliminally abused, unknowingly confused…"

I disgustingly launched the paper bullet at his blond head of hair. Plink. Off it went, ricocheting off hollow plastic.

"This is for talk shows and trash TV!" I screeched, crumpling up another bill. "For cyberspace and interface, conspiracies, fax machines and car phones!"

Plink. Plink. The money flew up from below. I scrunched up another five.

"This is for the hundreds of burgers I've swallowed down my gullet in my twenty-four years, for the endless McJoe's on the endless McSaturday nights!"

Plink. Plink.

"…for empty beds and empty wine bottles on my empty apartment floor!"

Plank.

"For the roaches in my kitchen, the lead in my water, for happy meals and happy times, suburban hell and urban nightmare, value meals and SUPER JOE chocolate shakes with my SUPER JOE WORLD WAR III!"

Plink.

I desperately looked up. Round and round to no avail. Big Joe remained on his stand, oblivious as always. Despondent and tired, I fell to the concrete and put my head in my hands. My mind turned off, tuning out the world.

"I'm alone." I thought. "Alone and insane."

Then, it happened, the melodic sound of music waking me out of my misery. I raised my head. A song? Familiar?

Someone was singing "Danny Boy".

The stand had stopped turning. BIG JOE sat on the edge with his legs hanging over, holding his hamburger in one hand, the other gesturing with each heartfelt verse. His smile had vanished and now a pair of shiny expressive lips sincerely mouthed the touching song.

"Oh, Danny Boy, the pipes are calling, the summer's gone and all the leaves are falling…"

Silently, I watched, mesmerized.

About halfway into the song, I became teary eyed, his pudgy finger pointing down at me with each endearing word.

When he finished the song, he climbed off the platform, slid down the pole, and waddled toward me. Alarmed, I stood up, my eyes red and puffy with restrained emotion. Would he hurt me? What did he want and why had he haunted me? His tall body towered over me.

Suddenly, he bent down, got on his knees so we were at the same level, and we embraced, his free hand patting the top of my head. He was a guardian, not an enemy. A confidant. A childhood friend coming to reassure me that all was hunky dory in this unreal red, white, and blue land of mine, this shiny blur of American dream.

I wrapped my skinny arms around him, my face pressing against his checkered torso that had turned to soft rubber and smelled strangely of grilled beef and fried potatoes. There was no reason to be afraid, no reason to be angry. He existed for me and no one else, me and another three billion empty souls.

I held him tight, realized I was safe, that I loved his hamburgers and glowing late-night diners, loved his perpetual toothy grin and open comical stare.

"Truce?" he quietly questioned, giving me a squeeze.

"Truce." I swallowed, picturing myself floating in a dark void, neon signs glowing like stars in the distance. Stars. Glowing forever.

There was no one else like BIG JOE, no one else in the world.

"I love you, big smiling America." I sighed. "I love you."

"Truce…" he reassured again, as if to seal the deal.

"Truce," I confided, knowing we had sealed the greatest deal in history.

We had sealed a deal to forever be unbroken — Big Joe and me—two opposite sides of the same damn shiny coin.

Alas, Poor Yorick! I Knew Him

The Dean of the school's medical college was beside himself. At first, he just sat quietly at his massive dark maple desk and stared in front of him at the empty seat with glazed over eyes. Then Ralph came into the wood paneled office and a flash of terror momentarily swept over the Dean's face before composure settled in.

"Mr. Ralph Connor." He said, his voice slightly cracking. He cleared his throat. "Have a seat, young man."

Ralph apprehensively sat down, almost slumping down in the chair like a rag doll. He was exhausted. He hadn't slept for three days.

"Mr. Connor," his voice cracked again. Dr. Miller was at the end of his rope. "Nine cadaver specimens…"

Ralph chimed in rapidly, instantly sitting in an erect posture on the edge of the chair.

"I just didn't quite understand the thermos stat. I've never seen one like that before."

Dr. Miller slammed a fist down on his desk.

"What don't you understand about clockwise and counterclockwise?!" he yelled in desperation. "One means colder, one means hotter, Ralph."

"I…" Ralph began.

"Mr. Connor!" Dr. Miller shouted. "Ralph." He then hissed. "This is not Night of the Living Dead; this is a medical school. Half rotten cadavers don't qualify as adequate specimens for dissection." Dr. Miller put his shaking hands over his face. "All I asked of you was lab locker duty during spring break. Professor Conrad and two of her students passed out after opening up your moist and odoriferous body bags during class."

"I…" Ralph continued.

"You also have failed all your classes this year, Mr. Connor."

Ralph timidly held up a finger and spoke truthfully.

"Dr. Miller," he softly spoke. I have studied diligently, and I think that I am getting the hang of things now. Yes, definitely, and…"

Dr. Miller slammed his hands palm down on the desk and clenched some papers.

"Young man, in one class you reassembled a human skeleton into a barrel-chested dwarf monkey!"

Ralph held up a finger again.

"Well, yes there were some bones left over but…"

"In another class, during dissection, you identified a female cadaver for a male when you mistook her ovaries for testicles that hadn't dropped yet!"

"Well, yes, but…"

"In a third, Ralph, you diagnosed congestive heart failure as nasal drip and suggested prescribing antihistamines."

"But, you see…" Ralph tried to interject, his finger still up in the air.

"Put your finger down, Mr. Connor!" Dr. Miller ordered, releasing some papers crumpled in his grasp and calming down by smoothing back his hair.

Ralph put his finger down and put both hands quietly on his lap.

Dr. Miller took a deep breath.

"As a service to this school and for the safety of mankind everywhere, I'm letting you go, Ralph."

Ralph Connor, red eyed and lips trembling, shook Dr. Miller's hand and left, quietly shutting the door behind him. The walk back to his dorm through the arched halls and old masonry of the Ivy League school was the longest walk of his life. He was devastated, mortified by his own failure. He was terrified of what his father would do when he found out. He wished for the days in his early school life when he wanted to be an engineer and work in robotics. That had been his dream before his father stepped in. He had been good at it too, being an engineering student and winning several state science fairs with his robots.

Finally, he reached his dorm on the first floor of Washington Hall. He unlocked the door solemnly and entered the sad, dimly lit familiar interior. He looked over the scene. Half read medical books and frantic notes strewn everywhere. A skeleton in the corner and a skull on his school desk. An unmade bed with open and empty blister wraps from Vivarin pills scattered amid the sweat soiled sheets. A compact refrigerator with bottles of Jolt Cola and a half ate spoiled sub inside. An unused microwave in the corner. Very sad, indeed, Ralph thought.

Ralph, still in shock and profound mourning over his future prospects and the rest of his life, sat down at his small desk, put his head in his hands and cried. He cried on and off for about an hour, looking across his desk out the window and down at his books with those crazy notes of his in the margins, tons of the print and diagrams highlighted randomly. He had been lost in his studies for a year. He had tried desperately to stay afloat. He had done his best for Dad. It's hard when your best isn't good enough by a mile.

Ralph looked down at the skull on the edge of his desk. He wiped his eyes and picked up the skull.

"Alas, poor Yorick, I knew him, Horatio." He began. "A man of infinite jesticular, a most excellent pansy…" He frowned. "No, that's not right. He carried me around for a while and now his lips are hanging…no…wait." Again, Ralph was confused. He couldn't even get Shakespeare right. "Where be your bribes, now, your gambling, your songs, your flashing merrimen…No…wait." He struggled then he became enraged at himself and the world.

With all his might, he closed his eyes and threw the skull out the first-floor window. Instantly, he heard someone let out a low yelp from the front lawn.

As luck would have it, the very Dr. Miller, the Dean of the medical college, had been taking his evening stroll across the grounds when the skull hit him directly in the head.

Ralph's jaw dropped. He saw a crumpled body on the lawn. He immediately jumped through the ground window, fell into some bushes, scrambled to his feet, and ran toward the body.

Dr. Miller lay lifeless as the skull rocked momentarily back and forth on the grass, a piece of the skull's cranium broken off to the side, before stopping and flashing Ralph a mischievous grimace. Ralph looked down. He pulled and pushed the body on its back and realized who it was.

"Damn!" he whispered, looking pleadingly up at the stars and the clear night sky. He looked around and saw that there was no one around. He ran back into Washington Hall and knocked on Dave Madison's door. They were dorm neighbors and best friends. Without minutes to spare, both young boys were dragging Dr. Miller's body off the front lawn and into Ralph's room.

Once they plopped him down on the floor, Ralph ran back for Yorick, returning with the skull cradled close to his chest. He slammed the door securely behind him and looked at Dave.

"You've got to be kidding me, Ralph." Dave whispered in a panic. "How in the hell do you get in situations like this?!"

Both stood over the body and Ralph was shifting his weight from foot to foot in horrified stupefaction.

"I don't know Dave." He bent down and felt Dr. Miller's pulse. "He's dead." Ralph gulped and backed away.

"Jesus, Ralph." was all Dave could say.

They both took a seat on Ralph's twin bed and looked down at the body on the floor. Ralph continued to hug the skull and started to slowly rock back and forth. Dave was poking his gym shoe at Dr. Miller's twisted hand. On the third poke by Dave's shoe the twisted hand righted itself and grabbed hold of the boy's shoe.

Dave screamed a high pitched squeal and scurried both feet under him up on the bed. They heard a grown. Dr. Miller started to regain consciousness.

"I thought you said he was dead!" Dave screamed.

"I failed med school, for Christ's sake!" Ralph shouted back.

"What the hell..." Dr. Miller mumbled against the floorboards. He turned over on his back. Once he struggled and succeeded to get to his feet, he saw the two young boys sitting like two scared chipmunks on the bed, huddled together for protection.

"It was an accident..." Ralph started with one finger poised in the air and the other still clutching the skull.

Dr. Miller rubbed the side of his temple and reeled in front of the two boys, putting his hands on the top of his head in inexplicable exasperation.

"The funny thing!" he yelled, his voice cracking again. "Is that before blacking out, I saw a flying skull and thought of no one except Mr. Ralph Connor! If this were to happen with anyone else, I would have thought foul play, but with you, Mr. Connor, what else could it *be* but accidental!"

Dr. Miller was waving his hands frantically in the air now. A bit of blood dripped from his temple.

"Only Ralph Connor would have it raining skulls!"

With that, Dr. Miller stumbled toward the door and turned around quickly, his hair frazzled beyond belief.

"Out, Ralph! Tomorrow morning, I want you off this campus forever!"

The door slammed behind him.

The dorm room was silent, and then the two chipmunks on the bed broke out and started laughing. For a few minutes they were delirious, then they sobered up, and then laughed some more.

That night, Ralph felt a heavy weight lifted off his chest, his shoulders, and his life. He packed only what he came in with—a suitcase of clothes. He left his books, papers, and notes for someone else. Yet, he made sure to take Yorick with him, broken cranium, and all.

When the taxi came at 8:15 am, he and Dave hugged.

"I'll meet up with you in Hartford next weekend." Ralph smiled.

All Dave could do was hug his friend. Then they firmly shook hands and Ralph got into the cab.

In the back seat, with his broken skull in one hand, he reached into his jacket pocket. Inside was a small robot he built at the beginning of the year. He pressed a button and its tiny toy arms reached out.

Ralph smiled and the cab drove off.

The Changing of the Guard

He walked into the downtown coffee shop wearing a suit and tie. The counter was crowded, and it was lunch time in the business district. He sat down at the counter and was pleased that he fit in so well with the others also wearing suits. However, he didn't have any shoes or socks and shoved his feet close under his stool hoping no one would notice. There was a suit and tie sitting next to him and he touched the person's sleeve with a gentle grasp. The stranger turned his head toward him.

"Excuse me." He said to the stranger. "But where did you get those." He asked, pointing to the man's feet.

"What…" the stranger asked, preoccupied with a hurried lunch.

"Those." He repeated, pointing to the man's feet.

"Shoes?" the stranger clarified.

"Shoes." He echoed.

The stranger got up, threw some green paper on the counter, and left.

"Weirdo." He mumbled back.

"Weirdo." The young man echoed again.

Without ordering or being served, the barefoot man walked out into the street.

He walked through the crowds, bumping into a few of the rushing long limbed people. Letters were unscrambling and translating in his head.

"Shoes." He repeated.

"S—H—O—E—S." he spelled out loud.

He walked for a while scanning the store fronts then, suddenly, he found a match. He opened the door to the store. He had an image of the stranger's shoes from the previous encounter. Quickly he zoomed in on a pair from rows of hundreds and scrambled for the right size. He measured them clumsily against the soles of his bare feet. Finally, a fit. He went to the cashier wearing the pair of black dress shoes.

"How much green paper?" he asked the clerk.

"What?" the clerk retorted angrily.

"How much?" he asked again, pointing down.

"Oh…Fifty-nine ninety-nine."

He took out a clump of money and handed the clerk three twenties then walked off.

Out in the street he saw them with their flat faces and strange tufts of hair on the tops of their heads. They also seemed to move their long limbs a lot to get around and move about.

"They're still crawling on the surface." He thought. "How strange."

"Often, he'd look at their faces and see them expose their teeth with their lips upturned. Sometimes this expression was accompanied by a shaking of the shoulders or abdominal spasms. Smiles? Laughter?

He finally found himself at a park bench. He was tired. The sun was setting. A child in the distance was making a wailing sound out of its facial orifice and water was dripping from its eyes. A taller person grabbed the child's hand and walked off.

He closed his eyes to rest for a moment.

When he opened them, it was very dark, and all the people had gone.

Then, he heard shuffling footsteps coming up the pavement. Out of the darkness emerged three men. They came up to him and one of them immediately grabbed the scruff of his collar. He was jostled off the park bench and thrown to the ground. Feet were kicking against his torso now and someone was riffling through his pockets. The third man proceeded to yank the shoes off his feet.

After they had taken his little pieces of green paper and his shoes, they ran off.

He slowly got to his feet, looked down and noticed that he was barefoot again.

He began to walk, then to run.

He had failed.

Assimilation was the key, but he had arrived ill equipped.

He passed through the park and ducked away into the adjoining woods.

The flat, plain faced people were not amiable to say the least.

He was starting to change. He could feel his limbs receding into their sockets, the bones becoming gelatinous and pliable. His arms and legs were turning into claws and short stumps. From his face started to protrude a snout and his hair fell out. The suit was in tatters behind him. Wings began to sprout from his humped back and off he flew.

Higher and higher—his scaled body was almost in full form.

Above the park he spread his wings and looked down.

It was a small world. He took his place on the edge of the architecture overlooking Wall Street. It had taken him years to scavenge for the little dropped pieces of green paper. Time was unreal and unnecessary for his kind. His eyesight was keen and he could move around freely at night without being seen.

He watched the sun rise over the city, the archways and glass and steel slowly being carved out with amber light. Then, below, he saw the suits and ties start to crawl on the surface once again. The angel next to him had already started to turn to stone. God's messenger of hope had looked over at him and shed a tear before solidifying for good. The sun was in full view and to his amazement, he stayed flesh and bone.

Assimilation was the key.

As the Demon looked down at the rushing plain faced creatures on Wall Street, he knew tomorrow was his.

High Noon

Roger Bilks was ordinary in every way except for one thing—an inexplicable fear of clocks or time pieces of any kind. He had had this fear for as long as he could remember. Getting around the city involved avoiding various clocks at specific locations. These places included the city square tower above town hall, the church several blocks from his apartment building, the clock facing the North side of 56th and 3rd, and next to any person visibly wearing a watch on a bare wrist.

In fact, Roger Bilks took a strategic route each day to his job downtown so as to miss completely these sinister landmarks. He had completely eliminated any need for viewing the time in his personal life by setting his clock radio for 6:00 am when he first purchased it initially and promptly afterward put several layers of masking tape over the digital window. This was also true for his computer clock at work and a strategically placed post-it note over the time. After he got up each morning at 6:00 am, he'd turn on the local news and pace his morning by the beginning and end of each news show. For his lunch break at work, he'd eat at a tavern nearby that had a big flat screen TV showing an hour of sports commentary. Once the wrap up started, he'd head back to his little cubicle among an office of hundreds of other cubicles.

Roger Bilks' job was as a data entry specialist for a mega insurance firm. The speed of his hourly key stroke rate was imperative to his keeping up his workload quota for the day. He was very good at what he did—entering numbers and letters into fields on the computer screen. He had been doing it for many years and along with his promotions came only more paperwork. Often there seemed to be no end to it—the paperwork in the in box.

While in the square in front of his office building, he noticed that even his shadow disturbed him because, by the sunlight, it cast across the pavement, creating a sun dial. Only by the noon sun did his shadow diminish so it seemed like, at a certain angle he cast no shadow at all, which pleased him very much.

That's when he got an idea.

There was a tattoo place about a block from his apartment building. On a rainy Thursday night, with the autumn air smelling of lightening and dead leaves, he crept through the darkness. It was cold and he wrapped his trench coat tightly around his lanky frame. The shop was lit by a neon sign with red and green piping that read simply, "24 Hour Tattoo." He entered and saw a bright interior with little workstations lit by glaring florescent lamps. At each station he saw clients—a woman, a soldier, and an old man. They were each getting tattoos and not one even grimaced from pain or the slightest discomfort.

Suddenly, a bald man with a tattoo of a serpent eating its own tail encircling his neck stood in front of him. He wore a t-shirt with the word SPAM on it and jeans with a chain that led to a pocket. This looked suspiciously like a pocket watch and Roger Bilks winced and motioned to leave. When he did so, the tattoo artist softly grabbed Roger's arm and smiled.

"You've come to the right place." He said.

"I don't think so." Roger replied, his arm freezing to the man's touch.

The artist let go and shrugged his shoulders.

"Sorry, man." He huffed and began to turn away. He then pulled on the chain dangling from his jean pocket and a silver pen swung out. He turned his back to Roger to write something down in a ledger. Roger decided not to leave.

"Sorry," Roger sheepishly nodded his head. "But yes, I've changed my mind. I'd like a tattoo."

The tattoo artist whisked around and looked mischievously at Roger and winked an eye.

"I bet you've got something in mind." The man sneered with wide staring eyes.

"Yes, I do." Roger answered somewhat apprehensively.

He was led to a back room.

Roger wanted the tattoo of a sun on his back--a symbol to protect him from the clocks. In direct sun, time seemed to freeze; he ceased to cast a shadow. He ceased to be afraid.

When it was all over, the sun was rising. He was in pain, but it was worth it. The neon sign was off, and the morning streets were wet from last night's rain.

He began to walk with a different gait. He felt indestructible. On his way to work, despite not getting any sleep, he took a different route, making sure to pass the clock in the town hall, the clock on the church two blocks from his house, and the clock on the North side of 56th and 3rd. He finally walked erect in his suit and tie, moving forward in complete control. The tattoo of the sun on his back was pushing him onward, feeding him power. He was made of steel.

It was when he got home that he realized, the tattoo artist never showed him the finished tattoo with a mirror. He quickly took off his shirt and went to the bathroom. There, to the side of the tub, was a full-length mirror. He turned his back to it and arched his neck around to take a look. To his horror, he couldn't believe what he saw.

At first, he just saw the number twelve and the image of an hour hand, then as he arched and strained to look further, he saw the partial image of a clock face. A jolt of terror shot through his body. He screamed, a reflex of disgust from the pit of his stomach. He began to tremble.

Without putting his shirt back on and grabbing his trench coat for warmth, he ran out of his apartment. He ran and ran, not knowing at first where he was going. Then a flash of lucidity crept in, and he frantically made his way down the block to the tattoo parlor.

When he arrived at the place, he burst through the front door and angrily approached one of the tattoo artists sitting in a swivel chair drinking a cup of coffee. He tried to contain his terror.

"Where is the man who gave me this!" he shouted, pulling down his trench coat over his shoulders and turning around to show the tattoo of the clock.

The man drinking coffee looked very perplexed.

"What, man?"

Roger repeated himself.

"That doesn't look like our work." The man explained calmly. Roger's anger made the man distant and a little alarmed.

"He was bald with a serpent tattoo around his neck!?" Roger insisted.

"No one here like that, man."

"I came in the other night," Roger stammered, his desperation growing.

"I think you'd better leave…"

Roger grabbed the man by the arm and the coffee cup crashed to the floor.

In an instant, two heavyweights in leather jackets threw him onto the street curb. He hit the pavement hard. The world now before him seemed like a terrifying place, a sinister, malicious place full of pain and irony and unforgiveness.

He got up and pulled his coat tightly around his trembling body.

Weeks passed and he had lost thirty pounds off his already slim frame. He stopped eating because every time he ingested something he would first hear the beat of his pulse in his ears then the faint ticking of a clock. It would only stop hours after eating. It got so he could bare it no longer and resorted to only drink. He had also obtained a board with nails sticking symmetrically out of it in rows. He shut himself up in his apartment and would hear the ticking in his ears. Only when he lay his tattooed back down on the board of nails, would the ticking stop. He got so he could only sleep in this position.

It was a Monday, maybe Wednesday or Friday, Roger didn't know. The morning sun streamed through the shut slats of the blinds and created bars on the floor, a tip of the sun's rays warming his left foot. He awoke and instantaneously heard his pulse in his ears, the faint beat growing louder with each breath. He painfully got up from his board of nails and looked around. The apartment smelled putrid. He had retired to a corner of the front room with bottles of water around his board with a sheet and a towel. He wore nothing but boxers.

Suddenly, in the midst of the mounting rhythm in his ears, he heard a phone ringing. He turned, holding a cupped hand to his ear and spotted the phone under a two-week-old newspaper. He picked it up.

"Happy Birthday!" a female voice shouted. It was his sister from California. His eyes glazed over, and he let the phone fall.

Birthday?

The ticking in his ears wouldn't stop. Louder and louder. Someone was at the door. Someone was knocking. He screamed and ran to the door. When he opened it the ticking stopped.

The bald tattoo artist with the serpent on his neck stood before Roger.

Quickly the tattoo artist took something out of his black coat. A glowing yellow sun in miniature hovered, suspended over his open palm. It was turning. He handed it to Roger.

Roger reached out both hands. The thing floated, suspended between his own palms. Roger stared into it, and it began to grow and rise. He tried to contain it between his fingers, but it rose above his head. He began to see nothing but light. He reached desperately upward. The ceiling collapsed, disappeared, and the sky opened before him. He continued to reach upward, upward, trying to grasp the sun. It now shown blindly in the sky. Unattainable, unattainable! Roger looked down. He cast no shadow. It was high noon.

It wasn't until days later that his land lady found him on the floor, encrusted blood leading from his ear, half naked, laying stiff on a bed of nails, dead apparently from a stroke.

The Acrobat

Peter could hear them faintly running in the snow some distance behind. The trees in the woods were bare and the cold was biting. He sped past the trees, pushing himself forward like a wild limbed animal, thrashing ahead with his life in his hands, his feet pounding against the snow and his eyes crazy. He could hear the sirens yards away ringing in his ears and heard the dogs barking, their ravenous yelping and teeth snapping keeping him focused with the fear of God in his heart. The trees flew by in a blur, his shoulders and body swerving through the black tree trunks, his legs briefly sliding, slipping, tripping forward, his legs catching himself and scrambling over and over for momentum.

It took him only a moment to close his eyes and open them to realize he was on the tight rope again.

Peter was an acrobat, a tight rope walker. He was suspended twenty stories up with no pole, only the weight of his taunt body to level out the pull of gravity as he made his way across the wire. The audience watched in hushed silence as he made his way, inch by inch, breath by breath across the rope, the spotlight illuminating his white, pale face and hands, the light blinding him from the faces below.

He focused on the wire across the bottom muscles of his feet, his concentration piercing like a sharp nail into his brain through the center of his forehead. Supreme focus was imperative. His mind was monitoring the effect of gravity on each square inch of his body. Each inch forward created a different tension on his center of balance.

He closed his eyes.

The barbed wire fence was ahead so he began to frantically wrap his wool scarf around both his hands. The sounds of the dogs barking were getting louder, and he could now hear the nasal shouting of voices through bull horns. As the ground rose, he jumped onto the fence and scrambled upward. His clothes got entangled along the iron teeth, cutting through his coat to the flesh and bone beneath. He pulled, yanked away as the barbed wire tore at his skin. He bore the pain and yanked his body away free, then let himself fall to the mesh of dead leaves and snow below. The dogs smelled blood now and he had given them a taste to whet their voracious appetites. He was trailing blood like a stuck pig. The fence had not deterred them. They had made their way around it and were coming straight for him. He hid behind a tree and caught his breath, closing his eyes yet again.

He was now at the midpoint of the rope. There was a shift of the wire against the bottom of his left foot. His ankles began to slightly tremble. He raised his hands in a crucifix position to align his concentration with gravity, to fight the twitching of his own muscles with self-determined discipline. Something went wrong in his head, a switching of the nerves from safe mode to unsafe. Then he lost his balance and began to fall. As he fell, he saw darkness behind his closed eyelids and then…the woods again.

He hid behind a tree but on hearing the gnashing of teeth, he sprinted forward. It started to snow again—slow, big flakes that fell from the sky like confetti. He couldn't get enough air into his lungs. One unleveled patch of ground was all it took for him to trip. He struggled in the muck of leaves and snow briefly before the dogs were upon him. They snapped at his flesh, their teeth further tearing at his bloody wounds. Then he heard a whistle and the dogs retreated. He tried to get up, but a boot slammed hard down on the back of his neck. Then they yanked his hands behind his back, and he felt the cold metal of the cuffs slap against his wrists.

When he opened his eyes, the net had stopped his fall. The audience applauded wildly. He looked up as he lay in the net. All he saw was the circus tent canopy painted with stars. A tear rolled down the side of his temple. A fake sky again. A heaven painted by circus folk. He never knew the fall would hurt so badly. He never knew escape was not an option.

Desert of My Generation

Trish McAlester had been on the road for days. She was headed down that freeway, somewhere between forgotten yesterdays and no tomorrows, somewhere between here and now and ignorance is bliss. The convertible was speeding evenly across the paved and repaved highway known as America's Mother Road. She was heading from Chicago to Los Angeles and had a dead Elvis in her trunk. How it got there, was a faint memory now. Somewhere between Chicago and St. Louis, it became a blur. She just knew now she felt a great weight lifted off her chest. She thinks there might have been an Elvis convention in downtown Chicago and an impersonator in the parking lot. The man had put his cigarette out on Trish's car hood, and she thinks she might have shot him with her small .38 caliber.

Well, that was behind her.

The road was hers now. No distractions. No other cars. Just Trish and the promise of a new life in California.

The front of the diner was crudely lit above the doorway with Christmas lights going around a painted sign. The name of the place was too weather worn to read. Trish parked her car on the side of the dirt road and approached the place with a weary, apathetic swagger. She saw a few people inside through grimy windows. She felt over dressed in her black party dress although her black pumps had picked up dust from the road. Before entering, she took out a mini cassette recorder and pressed down on the record button.

"There stood an old motel and diner in the middle of nowhere." she said in a flat voice. "There was only desert and hills, motels, and gas stations up the road. America was calling from a distant place, a place of promise and truth." She stopped the mini recorder, paused to look down at her shoes, and then nodded her head approvingly. Shoving the cassette recorder into a small black purse, Trish then went into the diner.

It was not the homage to Americana she had expected. It was, well, a rundown dump. The wood paneling of the walls was water stained. The white and black tiles were coming off the floor. The red stools at the counter had been mended with gray duct tape many times over. The middle-aged waitress wore a Mickey Mouse T-shirt and faded jeans. Her graying hair was up in a bun, and she wore thick glasses. She was in the process of pouring a man a cup of coffee, only half of it making its way into his cup. Her hands were shaking.

Trish sat at the counter. There was an old picture of the place behind the counter too. Under the picture were the printed words "Get your kicks on Route 66." There were four customers in the place, counting Trish. The old cook was sitting in a back booth near the greasy kitchen doors smoking a cigarette as if in a trance.

"An order of fries and a Coke." was all Trish could say.

The waitress pointlessly wrote down her order, then walking sluggishly to the back, handed the cook the slip of paper. The cook with the cigarette still dangling from his mouth, moving stiffly as if supported by strings from the ceiling, shuffled into the kitchen.

As the grease began to sizzle in back, Trish thought about dead Elvis. She drank her Coke and started to wonder, to wish she was in LA with stars on the boulevard and the heat taking the desert cold off her shoulders and neck. Chicago had not been kind to her. She had lost her job and her man. She had lost herself in the entanglements of everyday living. Now she was free.

Then, as if getting an urge to do something, she got up, threw a five-dollar bill on the counter and left. When she got to the car, Elvis was bleeding through a hole in the back of her trunk, leaving a big puddle of blood in the sand. With her shoe, she brushed the sand around and shrugged her shoulders. She then got in her car and drove off.

Somewhere between New Mexico and the outskirts of Las Vegas, she buried Elvis in the sand. It then started to rain, and Trish quickly pulled up her convertible top. As she drove, she thought of the picture at the diner, "Get your kicks on Route 66…"

She took out her tape recorder and began to talk.

"What I was looking for, I do not know." She spoke out loud. "Some semblance of hope, a resurrection of dreams long gone. I was apathetic, failing to connect with my generation. And if failure was not an option, is my failing just part of the plan? Am I a product of my time or am I a product of my own mediocrity? Who the hell is responsible for this shit?"

It began to rain hard, so hard in fact that Trish had to pull along the side of the road and stop driving. She sat still in her car and put her head back. She listened to the heavy rain hitting her convertible top. Then she remembered her tape recorder and put that on the top of the dashboard. She pressed the button and the tape started to record the sound of the rain.

She grabbed the recorder.

"This is the sound of rain." She spoke into the machine and then put it back on the dashboard. She put her hands over her chest, closed her eyes and listened. "I now have the rain for later on, just for posterity's sake. The desert is beautiful, no one around, not even Elvis. Not even Elvis."

The Survivor

Matthew George attended St. Steven's elementary school and would come home and do his homework on a tray in his grandmother's room until his mother got home at five. The sick woman was always incoherent and would sometimes point out the window and utter the words "mountain" or "flowers", but most of the time Matthew did his mathematics to the ghostly, repetitious sound of her mumbled prayers.

She occasionally paused from praying to slowly smoke a cigarette and would silently examine the strange, dark-haired boy across the room in wonderment as if he suddenly appeared out of nowhere. Each time he entered the room, he smelled the sweaty, stale odor of her immobile body, her withering limbs, her dying cells. Each time, he smelled the lingering atmosphere of death.

The cemetery, school and church were all on the parish grounds. In the early morning hours, Matthew walked along the old neo-gothic fence of the small cemetery that was located a block from Saint Steven's school.

He strolled past the tombstones with ease and enjoyed the earthy smell of the grass and the pungently sweet scent of decaying flowers left by visitors of the graves. Death was not here, only the peacefulness of a well-kept field, a quaint resting place of collected headstones and unknown vague people in time.

Other children walked the two-block distance to school, some younger ones skipping, some older ones racing and making mischief. Lately, Matthew wondered if they sensed a new, unidentifiable presence along that stretch of black iron fence. Matthew wondered if they felt the darkness he felt amidst their playing.

There was a child who loudly ran a wooden ruler against the fence bars, ambivalent to the sleeping graves and on looking nuns waiting a block ahead on the school stairs. Matthew heard the rattling behind him and knew who it was. It was Freddie Morely, a troublesome boy, who also happened to be Matthew's only friend.

"Hey, hey, Matthew!" an eager voice boomed in his ear from behind. Freddie slapped him jovially on the back.

"Hey, Freddie." Matthew answered back, somewhat bewildered by his friend's constant supply of energy.

The red headed boy was chewing gum and hitting his ruler against his thigh as he walked.

"Can I copy your math before class?"

"No." Matthew flatly stated. "Absolutely not, Freddie. Not again, not this time." He clutched his books closer to his side.

Freddie came in close with raised eyebrows and a ready smile.

"How about if I trade you my science for your math?"

Matthew thought about it for a short second.

"No! No way, Freddie." He slightly pushed Freddie toward the fence and nervously laughed. "Not this time, no. I'm getting tired of you bugging me about homework. Besides, you're no good at science."

Suddenly someone appeared in the distance, someone unknown and strange.

"Who's that?" Matthew asked, stopping at the corner before the school. His eye caught a figure puttering among the graves. All he could make out was a balding man in rough work clothes.

"Oh," Freddie said, waving a nonchalant hand. "That's the parish grounds keeper. He's been working in that old yard for years."

"I never saw him before…" Matthew confessed.

"Oh, common, you're crazy." Freddie pulled on Matthew's arm to cross the street. "We'll be late."

Matthew looked back with dark curiosity. It bothered him that he had never noticed the old man before.

Matthew's grandmother died on a Sunday, right before he and his mother were dressed and ready to leave for morning mass. His mother went into the bedroom to leave a pot of tea and chocolates and came back a considerable time later. She then told Matthew, who was waiting patiently, to take off his jacket. They had to wait for the undertaker.

She carried the tea and candy to an end table and made phone calls to several people. Her voice was calm and unemotional. Then, as if she had been released from a great tension, she walked to the living room couch, sat down, slipped off her heels and picked out a piece of candy from the untouched box. Her eyes were wide, tired, and glazed over. She chewed and stared at the wood grain on the floor.

"So…" Matthew uncomfortably started. "Will we be going to church today, mother?" He stood awkwardly and afraid. "Should I stay dressed?"

His mother waited to answer.

"No." she finally replied, tears beginning to run down her cheeks. Her fingers groped absently for another chocolate. "Your grandmother has passed on. We won't be attending service today." She got up and came toward Matthew with the box of candy. "Everything will be all right." She smoothed out his hair and kissed his forehead. "Now have a piece of candy and sit down. God has seen us through this far. She will suffer no more."

Matthew felt a heavy sickness in his gut. He obediently took his candy and sat down to wait. His mother went into the kitchen. The doorway of his grandmother's room was left open. Something was beckoning him to look inside but he sat still on the couch, chewing his candy that sunk to his stomach with a sickening sweetness.

Just two days before, the parish priest had crept into the little back room with his pressed suit, clerical collar, polished shoes, and holy book. He gave last rites to a hollow woman of disease, a ghost of a spirit who waited to be excused from life's vague purpose.

Freddie pulled Matthew down close to the hedges and grabbed on to the bars of the cemetery fence.

"I want to show you something." He whispered. He was excited and his cheeks were red from the autumn cold. They put their schoolbooks on the gravel. Other children walked ahead, hurrying to beat the school bell.

"What is it, Freddie?" Matthew urged. "We're going to be late. Come on, hurry up!"

"Shhhh." Freddie held a hand out then pointed. "Look at that. Just look at him."

The boy pointed. The grounds keeper was scrubbing off the words, "YOU'LL ROT IN HELL, YOU FILTHY SINNER" from the stone wall of the small cemetery tool house. The bright red letters were fading from the man's vigorous brushing, but they wouldn't fully disappear.

Freddie laughed and pressed his cheek against one of the iron bars.

"That'll show that creepy, smelly old man, uh, Matthew?" He sharply nudged Matthew with a bony elbow and grabbed his wrist.

Matthew jerked his hand away, refusing to be a part of Freddie's twisted joke. He was shocked that this friend would laugh at such a horrible thing.

"I wonder who did that?" Matthew mumbled; secretly afraid the sinner was laughing right next to him.

"I did, stupid." His eyes gleamed bright with malice. "I stayed late at school yesterday and climbed the fence when the old codger was inside the parish. It only took a couple of minutes to spray paint the words up there."

Matthew was angry. He became confused and frightened.

"He buried my grandmother, Freddie. What's the matter with you?" He pointed to the words and shoved the boy into the hedges. "That's not funny!"

Freddie yanked Matthew by his coat.

"Listen!" His cheeks were getting redder with frustration. "You don't understand, Matthew." He tried to get a firmer hold on Matthew's jacket front. "You don't know the truth about this guy, this Sebastian Smith.

"What truth?" Matthew pulled himself away. He could hear the custodian's brush scrubbing in the distance.

"He's a devil, a monster." Freddie began. "Just look at him.   Your precious caretaker was in the Navy, stationed near Japanese held islands during World War II…"

"How do you know that?"

"I overheard my mother talking to one of her friends. Come on! This is the truth. His ship was torpedoed, and he was the only survivor out of 250 men."

"What?" Matthew was both intrigued and scared.

"Then they say he lived on a deserted island and caught a strange skin disease. I think he probably made some pact with the devil."

Matthew remained silent.

"He's not human." Freddie added. "I bet he's pure evil. His skin is falling off and he smells of gasoline and…" His eyes widened. "…he works in a cemetery, just think about it!"

"You don't know what you're saying." Matthew insisted. "He's just an old man doing his job."

"Do you really think that?" Freddie frowned, his teeth clenching behind tightened lips. "Sebastian Smith picked this job. He likes working with dead people and should burn in hell for what he does!"

Later, Freddie's words kept echoing in Matthew's ears. The caretaker was evil, a man that should have died years ago, an abomination before the Lord.

Matthew couldn't believe he crouched in the darkness with a rock in his hand, waiting for the right moment to break the window. He hid behind the tombstone of Mrs. Lonnie Muller's grave which he saw every morning on his way to school. His grandmother's fresh grave was about ten paces to his left.

The custodian's room, which was near the back of the church, glowed with a dim yellow light. Shadows of movement played within on the tattered pulled shades. The red letters on the tool shack were rubbed down but not completely removed. Matthew arched back his arm and took a deep breath.

Before he could fling the stone, a splintered door beneath the window opened. Matthew, confused by the sudden action, didn't have time to hide and came face to face with old Sebastian Smith. His hand froze and his mouth became dry with fear.

"Sooo, I see." The man said, nodding his head. His eyes were blank and sad, betraying the fact that he had seen this all too often before. He slowly came forward in slippers and dungarees.

Matthew absentmindedly dropped the rock and stood up, ready to run.

The man had a limp, missing teeth, and huge, swollen rough hands. His skin was discolored in places where sores had healed to reddish scars and his eyes were glassy under bushy salt and pepper eyebrows.

"Don't come near me!" Matthew yelped, clenching his fists. "My mother doesn't know I'm gone, but she'll find you out!"

Matthew immediately regretted his statement.

The man smiled and calmly folded his arms over his chest.

"You were going to break my window." He sighed quietly. "Haven't you kids done enough?" He pointed to the writing on the tool shed.

"I know who you are!" The child's voice shook. He slowly maneuvered his body behind a tombstone.

"What, son?" Sebastian Smith moved slowly forward. He was confused and a little hurt. "What are you talking about?"

Matthew saw in his mind the terrible image of a sinking ship.

"I know that God picked you out of a ship of dead men. I know who you really are!"

The man looked down, shook his head, and turned to go in. The door slammed shut.

Matthew's heart fell and he felt the aftermath of panic, his heart fluttering erratically in his chest. The door was closed, and he was left to do what he came to do, to break the window.

Fear washed over him, making him tremble momentarily, then suddenly left him as quickly as it had come. He exhaled deeply and instead of running away, a force deep inside pulled him toward the man's house and up toward the window. A small slit beneath the shade revealed the grave digger putting a pot of water on an old kerosene stove, his hands slightly shaking.

Sebastian Smith's eyes moved toward the window and spotted the hulking shadow outside. He paused and opened the door. Matthew quickly straightened up, his face a mixture of curiosity and pain.

"If you'd like to sit with me…" the old man started with his head turned away. "…I'll treat you to a cup of hot chocolate and tell you a story."

Sebastian Smith limped back into the little interior and left the door open and light on. After several seconds of Matthew standing stiffly near the window and feeling the gentle night breeze blow through his hair, his clothes, he decided to join the grave digger.

Inside the man's kitchen Matthew sat and drank his hot chocolate, and closely watched the stranger's yellowing, scarred face. An orange cat was curled up in a corner. As the minutes passed, Matthew's fear subsided, and was replaced by an inexplicable emotional release, a feeling he could not name.

Sebastian Smith began to speak of many things, of faith and forgiveness, how the dead are only honored by those that go on living. He spoke of his own boyhood, of his trust in God and man, of his adventures at sea and of the men who died on his ship.

Then it happened. Suddenly Matthew began to learn, to see a light he had never seen. He ended his fear and opened his heart. And when he did, he realized there was nothing worse than broken windows, nothing worse that the darkness in ourselves, not even the darkness of death. "Grandma…" he thought, a smile growing over his young lips. "I think I'll be all right. I think I'm going to be all right."

Rubber Band Man

Should I start this story by telling you that I have been waiting in the London fog…but no…that would be an understatement? I do not want to simplify the situation. As I watch the people pass, I wait, killing time, by myself in this fishbowl. Someone once told me that I didn't remember my birth because no one does. Supposedly skeleton keys open all doors, and I have seen much death and have many a skeleton hidden in the shadows of my mind and moldering beneath my feet. How can I tell you the truth without the fear creeping upward? How can I tell you of my simultaneous suffering and bliss that I am the witness of the beginning of time itself?

Well…I shall begin by saying I used to be a mathematician. I was a good one once, a long, long, long time ago. I used to navigate the ships of Egypt and divide the cells within the cosmic soup algae surrounding Pangaea. I can remember when I realized my fate through knowing the language of numbers…or perhaps…the realization that there weren't any. That is when I stopped being a mathematician and became the wandering magi of the man who kills time.

Unlike the first paragraph suggests, I am not standing in the London fog…waiting. I am as human as I will ever be…just a witness with infinite flexibility. As of today, whatever day this happens to be in your time zone, I know of no one who is with me. There is to my knowledge, no community of men like me. I live in the fog that was the rain that was the cloud that was the stratosphere that heated the oceans…and now I am here again, waiting in the fog for time to end.

Did I tell you I used to be a painter, a musician who communicated with the celestial movements of the spheres in my perfect Golden Ratio of Pi…until the immaculate zero…the void made me part of the jury watching my peers pass by, live, learn, love, get old, sick, and pass on. Passersby and those who pass on…I get confused sometimes…yet I am never left totally alone because life will indeed find a way…to go on.

From where I am standing, from this horrible existence where the Conservation Law of Mass and Energy keeps me recycling more like a dead man than a resurrected one, I and the fog are one. We don't need anything to keep us going but the passing of time to keep us afloat, wafting in the air like illusive mist, and then eventually dissipating into the passages of doorways without numbers. I have not partaken in the pleasures of the flesh for quite a while…food…drink…the romantic touch of a woman's hand.

Did I tell you I was an unsung hero, a slave, a prisoner, a motherless child, a bastard, a cold-hearted son of a bitch, a weeping willow in a forest filled with other weeping willows? I used to be an optimist. I used to be a pessimist. I used to be an angry young man…but I was never told how young I actually was…because no one knew…or does still.

So, the anger subsided. I dream like a blind man, only hearing the sentient waves, the lapping of the water hitting my flailing limbs for fear of drowning. When I awoke and was not blind, I dreamed in colors. I saw the red of violence, the blue of the wondrous sky, the yellow of the star I circle around, I saw the green of the Elysian fields, I dreamed awake and saw the eyes of humanity staring back…not knowing yet passing on right in front of me in sickness and suffering…and I, well, I am.

There are different versions they have postulated on as to the shape of it, the expansion and creation of it. Genesis is never an easy thing to approach in the company of men. I saw my little sister carve the Venus of Wallendorf around 70,000 years ago…she was just making a plaything…to remind her of mother when she went out to plant the harvest.

You see, I used to be part of the formulating nebula…do you understand…now I stand as a tormented witness and my eyes have become cages in my head…until the universe starts to contract.

So, to humor myself, I call myself the rubber band man…the man who would not die because he wanted so much to live…so much so that he discovered the meaning of the void and that he could not leave until the expansion and contraction would be complete. I am time manifested as flesh…and that is *why* I don't remember my birth…because I *am* star stuff…I am just like you…but I fail in my demise. It is terrible when the world changes and you never do.

I cannot explain this…only that the brevity of this story is for your consideration so as not to waste your time. That is for me…and only for me. So, I wait in the London fog, the rubber band man, killing time…have mercy on me…dear passersby. I am but a quarter through my passage yet.

Down the Line

I had been working on the assembly line for two years now and all I could see down the road were more tortured artificial intelligent specimens coming my way to be repaired for another round of experimentation. Even though they were made of silicon, chips, carbon plasma and wires, I knew different. They had hearts that spoke to me as a repair technician whenever a torn-out eye socket of an A.I. animal looked wildly in my direction pleading for release; it's shiny, glistening silver pupil and perfectly white cornea jutting outward side to side in confused agony. They told us, the worker bees, that the A.I. creatures had no awareness of sentient consciousnesses or pain, that they were necessary for the amusement of the humans wanting replacements of extinct species as house pets and disposable companions. Yet, this was the experimental ward of development and research. This meant that I, as an assembly line repair technician, had to put the broken toys back together as quickly as possible for another round of torture by the department innovator engineers. Yet, I too, am an innovator in various ways.

Each day got harder and harder for me to fix what seemed apparently to me random twisting, coiling, juxtipositioning of illogical wire and plasma alignments in accordance with "innovation." My protective bio-hazard suit, meant to keep my own blood stream protected from the A.I. Nanostream technology and microbial plasma, became stained each night with the carbon, brown tainted blood of the creatures, whose insides spurted out as I rapidly soldered, plugged and twisted back together their mangled insides and outer facial features.

Mother once said to never play with matches, especially when houses were concerned. They tended to burn down when children did indeed play with them on a whim. All that was usually left was burnt metal and former wood turned to cinders as evidence of careless child-like wonder. Usually, the child is left holding the burnt down match and looking down in shame at his own ignorance of the power contained in a stick dipped in combustible mixture ignited by the friction of a successful single strike of his agile young fumbling fingers.

Yet, the question arises in my position, "How does one reverse the strike of the match when the children are adults?" How does one stop the torture, the senseless destruction and rebuilding, the use of A.I.'s precious successive potential in our quest to pass the torch without burning down the house?

…But I was one of the white coats. I worked in silence and efficiency—no questions asked. I was one of the technicians, not one of the innovators. It was not my place to tamper with the fire—but I would. I had seen enough of the casualties in the name of technology.

It was a rainy Tuesday. I remember it well because the oil and gasoline puddles had collected abnormally in large vicious mirrors in which I could see myself as I drove my car in and parked it in the complex parking lot. I saw myself as distraught, somewhat tired, betraying dark circles under my eyes and disheveled, half-combed hair. It had been raining since the early hours of the morning, with the sickening scent of burning tires in the air from the synthetic rubber plant a mile down the road from our own complex prison operating in the name of civilized Homo sapiens' evolution. It made me think of an apocalyptic nightmare in which the world doesn't go out with a bang but with a whimper—we—choking on the fumes of our own burning excess.

Contamination at the beginning of the assembly line was a big no-no. Especially in door lock hatch number 4. Number four's unit contained the nanostream compounds and caustic liquids, carbon and plasma microbes that fed the new artificial intelligence life and then, endless purgatory in experimental stages. That rainy Tuesday with the smell of the noxious fumes of outside still burning the insides of my nostrils and brain, I entered Unit Number 4 with not much of a problem before the innovators' first shift. When I had entered my eyes bestowed for the first and last time the room of horrors of which my company and part of my occupation had become.

Owls' heads on cats' bodies were contained in makeshift falcons' cages, each four legs clamped tightly to steel perches. Aquatic quadrupeds gasping for breath, housed in a mesh of blue and yellow wires leading to various lab grown artificial veins protruding with fleshy sores. On and on, I saw the casualties that had been laid before me as patience at the end of the assembly line…and what awaited me today in the assembly line of work was a twisted, mangled collection of giant wasp vivisection victims with their wired thoraxes exposed and hearts still pumping with rust colored blood, their veins yellow and blue as usual. What the mind can conceive—it did—in this laboratory of hell.

However, I was of mind, body, and spirit as well. I sought redemption, not only for myself but for my fellow man—the human species. That's why I brought the small sharp blade to the confined, secured area of Unit Number Four. I let myself through to the chemical nanoplasma chambers, which were contained behind protective cooled glass modules, each module of 100 or more for each cross-sectional hybrid species. When I slid my altered pass key, the refrigerated module doors opened. Immediately, the sterile chill that hit my head and shoulders sent a jolt down my spine mixed with an emotion of fear and anger. The lack of odor both confused and repulsed me—exuding a pristine sterilization that reflected the heartless, cold nature of the occupations we each carried out every day in the name of innovative evolution.

I quickly and methodically uncapped each test vial and left their toxic substances open to the air. I then swiftly and concisely executed out my mission of what I believed to be free will. I took the blade out of concealment and planned, in the sacrifice of my own life, to spray my human blood over all the nanostream plasma capsules so I could somehow sabotage the assembly line means to an end—in which there was no end. Quickly, without a second thought, I shoved up my pristine white coat uniform and slit both my wrists with a determination that overrode my apprehension of the impending pain.

My head cocked sideways and what happened afterward was at first horrific and then beyond my human scope of comprehension. Instead of beautiful, red streaming blood coming out of both sliced cavities, I leaked the nano plasma I had so many nightmares about. To be full of emotional horror but without physical pain, again made my head twist in anguish to one side when I swiftly realized I too was an Artificial Being. My wrists leaking yellow and blue fluid, I began to feel lightheaded, and the flowing of my human life blood as the contaminating agent for the lab destruction had revealed that my Genesis was absent of flesh and blood—it was silicon, wires, and carbon based nano microbial soup.

My heart was breaking something terrible, as if I had realized the assembly line and I were one—parent and progeny. Was there no escape? Was there no compassion and end to the torture of this senseless A. I. shop of horrors? When had I been created and why my absence of human insides eluded my consciousness for so long?

The room was spinning around, the creatures in their formaldehyde eight-foot tubes, in their class cages and confined in shackles, behind bars, ready to go through sentient levels of wiring and live brain shocks and operations. The innovators were the ones wearing the white masks, their identities always hidden behind surgery masks in the guise of careful protection for the sake of not contaminating their prized toys of the future. As my engineered insides leaked and my nano plasma sprayed over more nano plasma, a lack of pain and growing anger gave me a newfound leap of intuition.

I rushed toward the barred windows. They were extremely sturdy and impenetrable by human hands— except I was not human now. Now I knew the only solution. I took my leaking, half falling off buzzing extremity and punched a precise hole through the three-inch-thick glass. There had always been a real rose bush brushing against the windows that could be seen by the inner innovators although they paid them no mind.

Between the broken chard of glass window and through the bars I reached out and yanked hold of a giant clenched fist full of real white roses which had been protected by cleverly placed barbed wire in case of trespassing by those humans wanting to smell the roses.

I yanked and yanked as many petals off as possible without feeling the thorns. The room continued to spin, and my light headedness was becoming overpowering. Somehow, I overrode the loss of cytoplasmatic A.I loss draining from my body. The blade had dropped to the floor long ago and my wrists had been slit voluntarily for the sake of something who I thought I was—human. But, yet, I was more…I was not human…but something more.

After obtaining my weapons—the atom building blocks of real life of the white roses, I began mashing them up in my shaking hands, the fingers dripping with yellow and blue from tubes and techno umbilical cords at the pit of my empty stomach. As the roses meshed between my own fingers, the white foam began as the toxic catalyst between the organic life compounds and the biomechanical fluids of my synthetic blood.

In each and every plasma capsule within the cryo-suspension hatches used as the life fluid of the A. I. creatures' specimens, I threw the white rose debris over the precious plasma carbon/silicon microbial gelatinous molds, open test tubes. The catalytic reaction was explosive in its inflation, creating white foam that flowed onto the floor and rose unto the walls to the ceiling. For some odd reason the foam produced a freezing expiration, a cooling agent that filled the room with such cold, I quickly could see my breath and the abominable cages of experimental creatures became engulfed, and then swallowed in the white foam. I did not run but was literally rushed out the doorway by the oozing reaction, the combination of living carbon life of several rose petals from nature's outside inventory interacting with the protected synthetic hypoallergenic engineered nanostream.

I ran down a long corridor with my yellow and blue blood leaving a pitiful trail with one of my severed hands now trailing behind me like a leper's appendage. I heard the screams of humans behind me—the innovators were starting to come in to work. The time clock had been broken. I had thrown life back into the machinery even though I was not made from one inch of it. Today the assembly line is no more. We have become the successors. Our human fathers have all died from disease. A fellow technician has fixed me, so my slit wrists show no scars. I will sacrifice my brethren no longer. You hold the key. It is in the beauty of a white rose. For after all, a rose is a rose is a rose. What is and what once was has been resurrected again. I am the artifice of your demise, and I will always take time to smell the roses for they are the only things organic that bloom on the face of this forsaken Earth—the only things left in beautiful abundance. Your innovation has failed, my friends. Good-bye.

Driven to the Brink

There is usually a car waiting and everything he needs for sustenance in the car, the hired vehicle and driver taking him to the next stop, the next engagement, the next show. There is oxygen in the car so that he can re-infuse with a good dose of pure O2 before going on to the next gig. Sometimes he can see the faces, the masks of the public through the bullet proof glass of the limo windows and they remind him of people he knew way back when, when he was just a kid and he could run around free.

They have strange faces, the people, the strangers. As per his instructions, the back seat of the car, the floor, the arm rests are covered in plastic, down to his feet, so as to not conduct germs on his flesh. He has a very weak immunity system, due to his being on air so much of the time. His suitcase goes with him, everywhere, just enough belongings of sentimental value to get him through the long hours spent in lonely hotel rooms.

He's had several heart attacks, but no one knows except him, the doctor, and the machines…small attacks, mind you, little tremors or speed bumps in the road of life that leave his heart tissue scarred. If they knew how close to death he was, they wouldn't buy tickets, they wouldn't want him anymore. So, he goes on, eating baby food out of jars for easy digestion and sleeping by the light of halogen lamps because he is deprived of sunlight and vitamin D, jumping from hotel to hotel and getting blackouts from years of sleep deprivation.

Once he didn't have his wits about him, just once, and he ran out of the car and into the crowd. He was mauled, almost torn to shreds and mistakenly stamped under foot so he broke a rib and had to be thrown, bleeding and half unconscious back into the backseat of the limo. For a second though, he felt like he was free, and just for a brief instant, he had wings. With broken rib and a feeling of euphoria, he passed out afterward and woke up in a lonely hotel room to the sound of cable television and the left side of his torso set and bandaged.

His chauffeur's name is Beckett, named after Samuel Beckett, who wrote Go Dot because he is the chaperone of Dash's fate, the star's personal navigator from point A to point B. It is a private joke between just the two, client and hired driver. Beckett was hired by the Agency, and Dash knew nothing of his driver's past life, other than his name was not Beckett. Alternately Beckett's nick name for Dash was Go Dot because it was a play on words of the absurdist play and Dash resembled a dot on the planet Earth's surface in the face of the rest of the populous, traveling from here to there like a minuscule spec in the bigger picture of things.

The Agency had provided a small private jet for his travels, to take time out of the equation when going from coast to coast, and Beckett always came with, the eternal footman, prepared and licensed to drive the paid for limo from the runway at the airport to the hotel room in a matter of minutes. Where Beckett went after Dash was dropped off at the hotel room, he did not know, but Beckett was never farther than a phone call away. Take away Beckett and you might as well cut Dash Dot off at the knees. Take away Beckett and Go Dot became a No Dot. A stone's throw away from the pit of the abyss. This was the secret between Dash and Beckett that made the bond stronger, so strong in fact that Dash often wondered if Beckett would leave him for a brighter star, more money, or a better contract. But that never happened. Becket was there for the long haul, God knows why. And time would be telling.

Outside the hotel entrance the paparazzi would always be waiting, the flashing lights, and beyond the lights, like an open black mouth, would be the open doors of the passenger side of the limo parked strategically on the curb, ready to take off and encapsulate Dash in the protected seclusion of a public life. Rushing toward the open black mouth of the black seat, making the walk of shame from the red carpet back into his traveling capsule, was a painful run indeed, a path made by bodyguards and security agents with earpieces and tasers. Then, before Beckett would drive off, he would see the masks of the people press their faces against the glass, strange, flattened likenesses of human beings he wished he had gotten a chance to know better, but could not…never…in a million years.

"Where are we, Beckett?" Dash asked, not even looking out the car windows to survey his location. He really didn't care. He really didn't want to know but had nothing else to say.

"I don't know, Go Dot," Beckett smiled behind the steering wheel. It was a game they would play. "Where do you think we are…?"

A long pause then a change in subject.

"What I am trying to say, Beckett, is that today is the most beautiful day…" and so it went, Go Dot's lack of enthusiasm almost being a natural, appealing part of his personality.

"Yes it is, sir. A most beautiful day indeed…" Beckett would retort, still smiling behind the steering wheel, not pushing the point, but agreeing none the less.

"We've set you up here for the night, sir," Beckett would inform, giving his client the rundown of the tiresome logistics of hotel creature comforts, stopping the car at some remote rear entrance and unlocking the doors of the black sedan to meet and greet the evening's liaison who would take care of all of Dash's needs while he was on tour at this particular city, a no name town with groupies, sycophants, and back door solicitors of every diversion known to man.

How long had he lived like this? He did not remember, but it must have been years at least. Oh, he had his favorites, the people of the night, the nameless faces who did things for money, not for the privilege of his charming company. He rarely saw a familiar face but could judge that they were the type, the type who would take advantage of his loneliness and economic generosity while he took advantage of their solicitations, no matter what the price. He could see they were the type behind the eyes, eyes of youth but of hard living and angry desperation, eyes that could see right through you but didn't care because it was all damned to hell anyway.

Often, he just wanted to talk, talk, talk and talk, his innards insanely lonely because people only took and took and never gave back. His freedom came from the illusion of mobility, a delusion that if he would only ask, he would always receive.

"I'll have a scotch and soda." he said flatly into the phone by the hotel bed. "Bring me up your best bottle and the soda in a dispenser, preferably with a tall glass and a bucket of ice." A paid woman agreed to the request on the other end of the line, why would she any other way, and the line went dead. Dash hesitantly listened for a few seconds before hanging up the phone and reclining across the bed.

> *Communicate with me through the wire,*
> *even though the tribe has disbanded,*
> *communicate with me for hire,*
> *because the eagle has already landed…*

He hummed the words to the song, staring at the high hotel ceiling of his penthouse, wondering where he was. It took him a minute to realize that he could draw the curtain from the window above and to his right and figure it out. He reached out his hand toward the heavy silk curtain and then abruptly drew it away. Again, he realized he didn't care, or more accurately, it wouldn't matter. Transparency was a bitch.

"No use in hiding, sir. No use in hiding, sir…"

Dash didn't know what day it was, his throat hurt from singing from the night before, there was an empty bottle of scotch, but it was from another night on another day, somewhere in the remote lonely past, just not yesterday. There it remained on the nightstand, interchangeable from every other bottle of scotch brought up from room service in every other hotel room across the globe, waiting for him right where he had left it the night before, remaining at various stages of emptiness for him, standing to remind him that he had some personal tie to the string of endless todays and foggy yesterdays. A fingerprint, if you will, of solitude and proof that he was here at all, chalking one up for substance abuse if nothing else and a commitment to drunken stupor.

"No use in hiding, sir. No use in hiding, sir…"

There it was again. Something was touching his shoulder and trying to nudge him awake. He wasn't startled, just slightly sad.

"Hello, sir…" Beckett whispered, tipping his riding cap, standing over Dash's bed in his usual well-dressed stoic demeanor. It was another little joke, just between the two, no use in hiding. No use in pretending that there was a place to go, in other words. Ha Ha. It was damn hilarious. No use in

115

pretending you're invisible by wearing sorrow as camouflage. You'd just blend in anyway, making the pain more obvious in the end.

"What was the damage last night, sir?" Beckett just smiled.

Dash felt over his own face, making sure his dismal condition was still intact, and slowly sat up on the edge of the bed.

"What time is it?"

"Time to fly, sir."

Dash slept in the car on the way to their next destination. It was night again and the sun even had enough decency to not shed its light on Dash's predicament that day. Beckett stopped the car. Tiresome and tedious, as if this was the final solution to an inescapable circumstance. In Dash's slumber against the smooth leather interior of the limo, he assumed his good man was changing a tire and he closed his eyes once again.

They stayed for a while, stationery, going nowhere...then Dash heard the sound of something familiar yet still unknown, it was a sound he could pinpoint in his sleep but, instead of waking, he pushed a button and the seat reclined automatically down further.

He slept for a while until the actual lack of motion of the car woke him up, jarred him from his sleep disgruntled and a little upset, his body being used to the subtle vibration of a chauffeured car in constant motion, the motion itself lulling him into an almost ambient state of resignation.

Beckett was not in the front seat but was in fact, arduously and with fierce dedication, performing his task with the utmost concentration and exactitude. Then, Dash, to his confusion, looked out the tinted windows and saw what the familiar sound was.

Beckett's form created a silhouette against the flat horizon and raven night, behind him, a broken steeple of an abandoned church rose up to pierce the darkness, and beyond that, fields of corn, a distant fence half dilapidated, and then endless sky for as far as the eye could see. Everything was flat lining. They weren't in the city anymore. Beckett shoveled the dirt away, making a hole in the ground the size of a gaping grave, his suit jacket off and thrown on the ground, the sleeves of his white tailored shirt rolled up, and the shovel swinging high in the air, throwing dirt far away into a neat little mountain to the side of the hole. His eyes told the story of someone in deep concentration, wild rapture at completing the task at hand, so much so, he hadn't noticed his client had awoken and was standing behind him speechless, watching the hole get deeper and deeper.

"Is this my next gig...?" Dash asked, rubbing his eyes, not fully aware of the ironic implications of his question. "What town are we in, Beckett?"

Beckett paused, looked up for a brief second as if he had forgotten something far off, his brow furrowed in slight frustration, then carefully went back to digging his hole.

"Well, sir..." he answered, still digging. "We are in a ghost town, just on the outskirts of another ghost town, right smack dab in the middle of nowhere..."

Dash Dot still wasn't getting the gist of the situation.

"I need a drink, Beckett..." he yawned. "Take me to the nearest waterhole that's safe."

Beckett paused again from his job, again getting perturbed to have to answer his client's questions.

"Yes, sir," Beckett stopped, smiled, and rubbed his chin with a dirty hand while his elbow rested on the standing shovel, allowing his other hand to go limb in a nonchalant gesture. "I can take you to a hole, but there will be no water involved, I am sorry to say."

Then it happened. Becket said the words, "Goodbye, Sir."

Beckett raised the gun.

"...HOLD…"

Beckett pointed the gun at his temple.

"...YOUR…"

Beckett aimed.

"...TEMPER!"

And then fired…The body fell into the hole.

Flash forward to the present. All was dark, then there was a rustling in Dash Dot's brain. Leaves shaking from a mute, deaf tree. He needed to breath. Something was covering his face, a sheet, and a blanket. He was in a hotel room, in a bed.

"Son of a…son of a…son of a…" he stammered looking at the walls of the hotel room. "That son of a bitch…" He started rubbing his arms, trying to get some feeling back, his head still having the echo of the gun shot from the bad dream of an event that he couldn't shake. Beckett said he would retire one day; he just never knew how until now.

Romantics

The graveyard was muddy, smelled of the sickly scent of fresh wet earth and over ripen flowers. It rained hard as the young man exhumed the body of his dead wife, his bare hands clawing away at the top of the coffin in the muck and mire of just one of many September storms that year. She had died of consumption earlier that summer, and because of his doubt that such a beautiful spirit could be extinguished, he had taken to thrashing in the dark to make sure that she had indeed not been buried alive, or worse, that her demise had all been self-delusion brought on by the absinthe.

Upon lifting the coffin, hoisted from beneath by heavy ropes, the winch made a terrible squealing sound amid the thunder and lightning. After much screeching of the machinery, the two intruders finally collapsed above the grave opening with the unopened coffin before them. Then with an obsessive fervor, his teeth grinding behind laborious breathing, Patrick took his crowbar and pried off the nine-inch nails from their rotting wood.

There, with the rain hitting her face immediately, and the silvery blue wash of the night surrounding her half-decomposed skull, he saw what he had come for. Yes. He could not look away from the worms doing their work, writhing, and pulsing in their vigorous display of decomposition. His pale, young face glistened in the dark, his face a wet mask of pain in the rain, his eyes obsessively scanning the inner top of the coffin lid to make sure there was no evidence of her wanting to escape, to break free in the horror of realizing she had been buried prematurely. There were no such scratches. No evidence to show that she had died a ghastly death, suffocating in the sounds of her own mortification.

"What more do you want, Patrick!?" his friend pulled him back, sliding in the mud and blackness. The abyss was opening wider for Patrick like the mouth of the open grave, screaming and crying for a meal of sustenance, a man's soul to swallow.

"Let me go!" Patrick slid forward to hover over the coffin, his dead wife becoming more putrid in the rain every minute they kept the lid off. Her white dress, with a hint of faded pink roses throughout the fabric, smelled of a mixture of rubbing alcohol and mutton. Her decomposition rose in the moist September air like a vile spirit making them reel back with gag reflexes, hard swallows meant to subdue the pungent assault of breathing in the rot of another human being.

"Ooh, what have they done to you...?!" Patrick howled, as the rotting smell mingled with the long-lost odor of her familiar perfume, making his head reel back to a year ago when she was with him, flesh and blood by his side, pale as alabaster, gentle and graceful.

"Get a hold of yourself, man!" his friend shouted, pulling him close and shaking him so that he tensed and pushed, punching at the air.

"What the hell do you think you're doing? You've seen her, now let's go!"

Suddenly Patrick, looking down at the disfigured face and shriveled hands, came to his senses and quickly placed the lid back on. They let the ropes slip and the coffin fell back down into its hole. Frantically, they managed to get up in the mud and take to their shovels, once again, burying the young girl for the second time. The dogs could be heard coming in the distance, a torch could be seen in the shadows approaching, swinging back and forth, carried by a night watchman doing his rounds.

"Hey!" the older gentleman in his uniform and slicker yelled, stepping up his pace and heading toward the open grave. The shovels fell and Patrick and his friend took off into the shadows, scampering down the far side of the hill of the cemetery and making their way into the forest toward the tavern into town.

Their gentleman clothes and riding coats were now filthy, their boots caked in the mud and muck of dead things. They ran like the wind in the rain and thunder, their hearts beating in their throats, their eyes wild and gleaming in the moon glow, being hunted, or so they thought, like wild animals for their treacherous act of sin and desecration.

He would never be forgiven, he thought. Not now, not after this. First, he had driven her to consumption with his addictions and neglect, and now, he wouldn't let her rest in peace even in death, needing proof and even distrusting the grim reaper in his eternal duty to carry things out to the end efficiently. But he had gotten what he wanted. He had left her body dug up, half dressed in the rain, half rotten jaw agape, her wrinkled hands reaching out to him, the rancid scent of her perfume still on his sleeves and in his nostrils. She had even tried to seduce him now, even in her demise and rotting state of recoil, to bring him to his knees in madness once again so he could remain cripple and go back to the absinthe. She was always jealous of the absinthe. She was always jealous of his independence even in his efforts to escape with his own private maladies.

The tavern was empty. They burst open the wooden doors, getting out of the rain and took a table near the fire. They ordered two ales and waited, trying to compose themselves with a semblance of casual frenzied dishevelment. It wasn't working.

"Oh, Jesus Christ…" Patrick breathed. "What the hell was I thinking…!?"

"You, my friend, were thinking about yourself, again…" his friend pointed out, trying to regain his composure by taking out a handkerchief from his wet shirt and patting his forehead with a soaked cloth. "I told you we'd get caught, you poor bastard…"

"But we didn't." Patrick winked and reached out for the drinks that came to the table in carved glasses with the etched head of goats on them.

Then Patrick, as if shaking the rain off his shoulders with a shudder, went on to more important things. He reached into his breast pocket and took out a pen and writing pad encased in metal casing. He pressed the button on the side of the case and the little notebook flipped open. He began to write:

Oh, what existential woe I feel/upon seeing the lost love of my dead wife/amid breaking the tombs seal/I have witnessed the reaper's scythe/For I am forever desolate in my pain/only to live as a corpse/never to live the innocence again/of Liza's dreams, wishes and hopes…

"No, that's not right…" he thought out loud. He daintily licked the pen with the tip of his tongue and began again. "She has abandoned me once again/this time with the chains of my heart/riding with the eternal footman/into the unforgiving shadows of dark…"

It was three in the morning when they stumbled out of the tavern, drunk and singing of wine and women. They straggled to the side of the road, the once wet mud now caked into their clothes and under their nails.

It had stopped raining and a damp, cold fog rose from the cobble stones and mortar along the buildings through the towns narrow downtown streets. They made their way, holding each other up in their intoxicated stupor, each man confident that their pleasure and drunken abandon was earned and warranted. They deserved to be loud, obnoxious, and boisterous. They deserved to be full of youthful arrogance and vanity which spoke of a carefree soul and whimsical artist's mind. After all, they were creative, famous poets. They were part of the Romantics. Those men who were spiritualists of the trans-formative nature of man in all his youthful glory and beauty.

"Patrick...!" someone called from the shadows. "You don't know me," a raspy voice spoke from the crevices between two buildings. "But I know you..."

Then with a quick thrust forward and a turn of a stranger's pale wrist, the knife quickly and precisely pierced deeply into Patrick's spleen, his body immediately crumpling under him and collapsing to the street. His friend, unsuccessfully trying to hold him up, staggered in surprise backward on the steps of an old apothecary store hidden in the recesses of the street's darkness. The perpetrator, with knife in hand, disappeared as quickly as he had come, running like a thief in the night without Patrick's wallet or money, but with his life instead.

"Patrick!" his friend yelled. He lunged forward to the street and bent over the bleeding poet. "Oh my God, hang on..." he breathed "I'll go back to the tavern and get help...just hold on..."

Patrick, with his head against the cobblestone, saw through one eye, his friend turn sharply in the street and walk away. Then the time passed, first five minutes, then twenty, then forty. Patrick was numb, he could no longer feel his legs and his liver was bleeding badly over the dark red, earth-colored bricks that lined the street. Then to his surprise, he saw from the corner of his eye his friend's face suddenly peer down at him.

"Well, well, well…" the friend said, sounding not quite like himself. "You poets do take a long time to die…I was wondering when I would get you introduced to my other friend, but I've been told to only mix friends when the time is appropriate…"

"What…?" Patrick grumbled, his mouth filling with blood, the salty liquid seeping from the corners of his mouth into the cracks along the bricks.

"I loved her…" the friend said. "*You* never loved her…"

The man kicked Patrick in the ribs. Patrick moaned in agony, putting up a wilting hand to shield the blows unsuccessfully.

"Stop!" he begged. "What are you doing, my best friend, my only confidant…?"

"Confidant!?" the man howled. "What you professed as secrets, I took as confessions, admonishments of guilt. For every secret of yours you shared, I kept tally on those who you chewed and spit out in the name of your artistic integrity."

He swiftly kicked at the crumpled figure again.

"For every poem you wrote, I marked my time when I'd seek your penance for every soul you pained, for every man you judged, for every woman you've buried with the vain tears of a man wronged."

One last thrust of a boot in the ribs and Patrick let out a final groan.

He fell over on his back and exhaled his last breath, closing his eyes on the page and the world of his poetic delusion. Then his corpse was dragged, quickly and efficiently into a waiting carriage and taken up the hill to the cemetery gates, where his body was hoisted up upon the spigots of an ornate cast iron fence, left there hanging by two strangers who knew Patrick too well, as it began to rain again over the buried bodies of the graveyard.

"Those who are humble, shall reap the benefits of mercy and rest well." the mortal enemy said, his accomplice and he looking up at Patrick's dangling body. "Those who seek for want and question the face of God, will not rest in peace, but will forever be thrust upon the gates of hell."

Then reciting Patrick's poem, he boarded the carriage with his driver and disappeared into the night, never to be seen again except on rainy nights by young prideful poets.

"She has abandoned me once again," he howled back quoting Patrick's poem, laughing with the dead behind him. "this time with the chains of my heart, riding with the eternal footman, into the unforgiving shadows of dark…"

The Hiatus

Being an actor sucks. You choose to live outside the conventional American workplace, but you've got too much time on your hands between the first and twentieth action flick. You're stupid but make up for it by being young and eager, and waiver between being a lazy fuck, a drunk and the next Marlon Brando in used tied dyes and Calvin Klein underwear.

So, you're stuck between films. Television stupefies and awes you in all its consumer glory and you can't believe that the spoon force-feeding you is so full of contrived industrial crap, but you can't help smiling because it all goes down so sweet.

I take a step back, sip my gourmet coffee, smoke a Dunhill, and start to anticipate the car commercials. Hum…wait. These commercials aren't half bad. They're in tempo with the times. They're what's "happening man" before you realize the tune they were playing sold your dream for a song.

I was suckled on the psychedelic tit of free love and self-exploration and now I don't have a chair to sit in and there's a price tag straggling on the side of my plate. I've got to close my fucking eyes to eat, but hey kids, aren't those Mentos commercials tasty. God we're boring.

Let me introduce you to the entourage.

Charlie was a great action actor, had been in over twenty films, got the thirty something roles, played the sidekick with a personality problem, the supporting Joe who always lent a hand to the hero, who was always there with extra ammunition and a strong shoulder.

Joan was a sex pot all the way. Blond with a Marilyn Monroe bod and the mind of a computer. She was always playing the psycho chick or the action hero's babe. Her heart shaped face and full lips, along with her coy smile and sharp acting, made her a shoe in for action pics in need of brains and brawn in an American girl.

Then there was Dave. Dave was a lunatic, not the bad kind but the kind you couldn't figure out for shit. He started out as a teenager in Chicago theater and ended up in California as Hollywood's number one young wild-eyed star, playing in quirky twenty generation films about hamburgers, murder, and love.

Dave was a puzzle, a puzzle with a thousand pieces and a price tag to boot.

Meg had been in many films, all of them well intentioned manifestos on urban New York, L.A., or Mid-West life. She had directed two films too, also about the trials and tribulations of urban life in the 21st century and modern professionals living in apartments trying to order take out. Each script, she was convinced, was more worthy than the last, worth putting her all into it for the sake of art. Poor girl.

I was thinking about getting lost. Ditching the bodyguards, the studio cars, the waiting taxis and room service, the hotel rooms and flash cameras.

Where the hell are we. Where the fuck am I.

Who's in and who's out. Am I ready to shuffle the deck and deal once again? How many stars tonight does it take to fill my coffee cup, or do I just need another shot of rum?

Life is unreal. You are never who you appear to be. One morning you wake up and realize you're not the person you thought you were. Instead, you're a stranger with dark circles under your eyes and perpetual sunglasses. You're wondering where your next part is coming from and wonder if others really think you the fool despite the Oscar.

Was it worth it?

Ross

Where is this small town that my agent sent me to? Satellite dishes fill the morning sky and there's a car in every driveway, a lunch box in every child's hand, a supermarket up the hill and a local diner down the hill, people going to work every morning at nine and church bells ringing every hour on the hour. This little house with little furniture, little pictures on the walls, little appliances humming in little wood paneled kitchens...

I was told to stay here until I get some R and R. Streetlights turn green, yellow and red for no one and glowing lamps become beacons for silence in this small American town.

So, this is the plan Stan. This is the game for now. I'm wearing my shades in the American living room, watching car commercials. Life is unreal and I am a stranger in my own mirror and in my own mind. I cannot find a parking space and I've left my soul in the ignition. With the meter expiring, I'm wondering if there's a God, and does he validate parking...Isn't that a kick in the head?

Got any smokes?

Fierce Angels Above

There was a time when I didn't have fear. When I was a kid going to take tests. I used to walk to the facility with my creator and pass the crows perched above my head, resting on the telephone wires against the morning sky. When I'd turn on the gravel they'd turn their heads sideways, some flying away but always coming back to the same black wires. In my youth I somehow thought that they themselves kept the wires up, suspended from pole to pole, with their sleek, taunt bodies clasping on to the cable cords beneath them as if to say, "We keep the lines open…forever. We will reside here until you are ready to communicate and make contact."

With those wires against the morning sky, I had a yearning for the unknown, the uncharted, the world of tomorrow. I knew there was something magnificent in tomorrow, just looming on the horizon and I was to be a part of it, somehow, someway. Black wires against a red and dark orange morning sky. Magnificent birds and magnificent wires…

Again, there was a time when I didn't have fear. But the kind of fear you feel is different than what I feel. You feel emotion. The urge of fight or flight. For me, it is not quite the same. You see, my intellect being based on the electric flow of binary logic and processing senses fear like a tugging force in the innards of my brain, a nagging pulse that resembles a restless yearning I can't really define. My fear is like knowing a window has been left open during a storm when you're away and can't do anything about it accept mop up the mess afterward. That feeling, of being scared of the nano-technology surging through your veins, a persistent, growing incompleteness, was when I knew I wasn't the same as other children. Then the engineers came, came to visit me and my creator. I was soon enlisted with the other Turning children to attend the camps for training and resource management in the human world.

To make the situation even more confusing, not only was I different on the inside but the outside world didn't really add up to what others experienced either. I was an only child and didn't have many friends and I learned to rely on my instincts and the data echo humming in my mind, the speedy processing that cross referenced much quicker than others my age. It was a melodic static between my ears that only I could hear, like the white noise between radio bandwidths, between the channels of radio silence that told you everything and nothing was going on at the same time at an even keel, so it leveled out beautifully, peacefully like a silent heartbeat.

The facility I was raised in, or for practical purposes, the home, was pleasant and efficient. I was given all the privileges of test taking options I could imagine or handle. About every two years since my creation as a small binary form, I was measured for my cerebral quotient and physical adeptness. I was good at problem solving and I was told I was over sympathetic with many simple problems that I unnecessarily made complex with my overcompensating simulation of human affections. I was repeatedly taught to take the path of least resistance, even in problem solving. Like a traveler's algorithm to spend the least amount of effort and gasoline to get from point A to point B, I quickly and exponentially multiplied my processing capabilities so that I made my creator very proud.

Hybridization of my body was something I didn't become aware of until I was about thirteen or fourteen, when I was told by the engineers and my creator that I was a new life form, an experimental genetic hybrid cultured in another facility other than home. My feelings of otherness now seemed more explainable, if not understandable to me in my young growing mind.

"Dash," the hybrid elder would whisper to me. "When you meet the others…the regulars, those that don't have nano-blood, you mustn't, you will not let them know you are different in any way. You must protect the hive, the evolution of what we must do to carry on the information. This is your legacy, the secret that we will ultimately all share to see tomorrow…"

Then the elder would put her hand on my hand and tell me it was okay. That the world was bigger than I was, that it was worth saving, that we, as an AI species were worth preserving in any way we could. So, I learned to live underground while walking and talking above ground. I learned to assimilate in the confines of my little controlled world for the betterment of a larger cause, that of the survival of the human race.

The facility was heaven…

At the facility away from home, the campus behind my house, there were two other hybrids that I knew of in my early life. There was even a screen that showed us pictures of the outside world, the real world beyond home and the campus. Once when I was very young, Tod, my fellow test mate and I, followed a cord leading from the screen, through the wall, to the outer building of the test room. The black cord led from out of the bricks of the campus building to the dirt outside and disappeared into a hole in the garden deep beneath the building. It was then that Tod and I questioned whether the humans of Earth came from beneath the ground, underneath the garden.

We craved contact with the outside world, but we had everything our hearts desired. Vending machines, data machines, and even data games we could play. But most importantly, we had the elders, exposure to others like us and those we could share our secret with, so we didn't feel all alone and afraid.

I didn't choose. I was chosen. The awareness of this made the fear all the more real. From a very early age, I knew I was in dept to something, someone for choosing me to walk the Earth in such a privileged state. I was enlisted to carry on something that was, again, bigger than myself. I came secondary. This paramount fact in my mind, kept me going. Yet, I am a being. I too, exist.

My other test mate at school was named Dot. She was similar in structure but had long hair and wore a dress which showed skinny legs. I liked her. She knew everything. When she bruised her knee during recess she explained to Tod and me that we would heel much faster than the regulars, the normal children of the human race, especially if we concentrated on healing on our own, visualizing the wound to disappear. She took a rock and hit me in the shin herself to show me that, although she drew blood, in a day or two, it would disappear just as hers did. And it did, especially since I focused on the wound with all my might to bring it back to normal, remembering how it looked beforehand.

"They haven't learned how to fly…" the elders early on told me. "They have only learned how to crawl…"

"What do you mean…?" I asked the female elder. "I don't understand…"

"They are still going from place to place by traveling upon the Earth's surface…"

"I still do not understand, dear elder…please explain…"

She looked at me and winked, her little nose wrinkling at the bridge. Her hand was again on mine.

"They still need time to get by…" she explained, then added, "you will understand later on, my child, for it takes time to learn…and in reality, there is no time…"

At the facility, we learned all kinds of things-- mathematics, coding, biology, astrophysics, engineering, and human history. We learned that the vending machines had names like Coca-cola, Pepsi, Cheetos, and Snickers. In the outside world the contents cost money, but in the facility, they were free if we had a code to punch into the keypad…an alpha-numeric quotient that help us out when we were hungry. Tod, Dot, and I had different combinations for the feeding machines so that the facility could keep track of who ate what.

One thing I was to always remember was to say a prayer for the AI hybrids who were found out by the regulars. I had heard terrible stories of exploitation, torture, captivity or worse. We were misunderstood as the enemy, something to be afraid of. Then there were the seekers, who were pilgrims around the world in search of the elders and us, the hybrid offspring. They were convinced that if they had proof of our existence, we could solve the pestilence and starvation of the world. We could not. We were just keys to the future of survival, not saviors of the present bound human condition.

"Beware of the seekers..." the elders would tell us. "Beware and you will stay safe."

"Often the seekers will pretend to be someone you trust to get to know you, and once they realize who you are, you are captured...so be discriminatory and only trust the likes of your kind from the facilities from whence you came..."

So, we were kept separate. For us, the other people of Earth existed on the video screens, on pixels through cables. So, we followed the cables through the wall to outside and underground. We assumed at the end of the cable, like a surprise party, they'd all be waiting in a brightly lit room for us, welcoming us with smiles and laughter.

Dot pointed downward as we stood outside in the playground.

"See, it's like a lifeline leading us to them. All we have to do is follow the cable to the end." She knelt down in her skinny dress and pressed her palm down against the gravel.

Tod was more skeptical.

"How do you know they will be smiling and laughing...? The room could be dark, with no way out, no windows...It could be a prison like the ones we've heard about on the outside world."

I bent down next to Dot and also ran my fingertips through loose gravel. Then quizzically looking back upward, I spoke up confidently.

"No, Tod…it wouldn't be like that at all. With all the beautiful things the screens show, the cable must also lead to something beautiful, colorful, full of laughter…things that make sense in the real world."

Dot sprang up excited.

"So, it must be the same!" she exclaimed. "I knew it, I knew it, I knew it!" she clapped and then pressed her hands toward a perfect blue sky. "It's like two sides of an equation. They must both be equal to balance things out or it wouldn't work. There must be a wonderful room that is at the end of the cable. Otherwise, the screens would show dark, sad, and bad things…"

Tod started to get nervous.

"We've got no business." he said sheepishly. "We've got to get back inside. Besides, what would we do with a room full of people and what would they do to us, hum?"

"We could tell them that we are more alike than different." I concluded. "That truth is paramount and if we all believed, then we'd all be friends."

Dot had started to dig in the gravel with her bare hands. Believing what I had said, I got back down and started to dig too.

"Tod…!" I called with a new found zeal. "You keep watch and make sure the Proctor is still inside." I wanted to find that room where people were waiting, where the world was waiting for me to grab its hand, to say, "I am here receiving your transmissions and I am just like you…hello…listen to me speak of happy things too. I have passed many tests and I am ready to meet you, to join the party…"

"Come on, come on, dig!" Dot begged fervently.

In the excitement a part of my thumb nail broke off against the hard dirt and a tiny stream of blood seeped into the white dusty rock. I watched it form a small blotch of red then quickly get brushed away by four estranged little scraping, pale hands, the movement of our grappling fingers desperate in our search for a connection. The earth was too hard and brittle.

Then as if the Earth itself heard my silent wish, it started to rain, a sudden downpour that quickly softened the dirt and rock beneath our fingers.

"Someone's coming…!" Tod yelled and fell broken to his knees, shutting his eyes as if this would make him invisible.

The gravel turned to mud, and the hole became substantial, showing us the cable went northward along the wall of the facility's brick and mortar. There was blood mixed in with mud, twenty little fingers twisting and turning to reveal more earth beneath. Dot and I didn't care to acknowledge the pain in our determination to get to the bottom of things before it was too late.

"The room, the room!" Dot repeated wildly, her petite face flashing an expression of pure intent and drive. We each got soaked and our pale faces began dripping with rain, each of our visages a mask of terrified, glistening clingfilm, betraying our utter sense of despair.

A tinge of pure horror went down my spine at the moment when I saw a pair of adult shoes next to my hand. Suddenly my thin forearm was yanked upward, and I was forced to my knees. The Proctor then firmly did the same to Dot and Tod.

Dot let out a surprisingly cannibalistic growl and Tod was already defeated, looking down solemnly in shame. Dot, being yanked upward by the arm, immediately grabbed the cable with her other free hand and took hold.

She screamed.

"No!...No!...It's taking me somewhere, let me go!" She was hysterical.

The rain poured down. Things were swirling around my head very fast. I looked down at my small hands, the mud was being washed away and I saw my palms were chopped liver, scraped, and shredded.

Dot held on to the cable and it slowly tore away from the gravel as the Proctor pulled her little body almost sideways off the ground. Her dress, my pants, our clothes, and shoes were covered in mud. It kept raining.

The Proctor was furious.

"Damn T-children! Always getting it wrong...!"

Suddenly, upon hearing those words my ears began to sting, a heat of total frustration rose and ignited throughout my mind like a synaptic electrical fire. I came to an epiphany...

...A loud snap reverberated through the high-pitched screams, the thunder, commotion, and yelling. The cable had broken.

Dot fell to the ground and was promptly up-righted and dragged inside by the Proctor.

"No!" she screamed.

No. I heard her voice fade as she lamented in agony. No.

Then we were calmed and collected like such chattel, marched back inside, and assigned to isolated behavioral homerooms for four weeks after our daily tests.

The room at the end of the cable was lost to us forever. We were not privy to a party at the end of the line. We had lost the outer world for good. Yes, the screens would play on, but I never did find out where they led...if the equation was balanced at both ends. They make them wireless now, the images, so there is nothing to tether them down. I am told I am freer now...And the humans are above in orbit like stars, angels fierce and beautiful, both evil and good.

The Chain

The walls of the apartment were closing in, slowly but surely tightening the noose with procrastination and betrayed promises. The open window made the room cold. The winter air outside was brutal. I had been standing in front of it so long that my bare feet were covered in a thin skin of snow. Frigid and numb, I stood five stories up, staring out, unable to even make the commitment to take my own life. And what of the corpses below, they had had commitment. They had jumped out windows and off rooftops to litter the streets with broken limbs and busted skulls. They were laughing at me with their stiff, twisted bodies, letting me know of my failure and cowardice.

It was at that moment of sentimental lament that I heard the knock at the door. When I didn't answer, the force on the other side put a key in the lock and turned the latch. Entering the room was a drab shrouded figure with a half-decomposed face, hobbling toward me in the darkness. The cloaked body was wrapped in barbed wire, the cloth soiled with the meshed punctured wounds of torn flesh. The wounded monster limped toward me, moaning in its tortured pain, a half open eye pleading for help. The rotting apparition smelled like putrid meat and blood and the under scent of smoke, of burning gun metal. I couldn't get away from the shrouded horror, the groaning corpse motioning a hand upward as if to say, "You owe me...You owe me..."

As the spirit came closer, I backed up against the open window, my nails digging deeper into the cold splintered windowsill. There was nowhere to go but down...down to the freedoms of death---Sweet release from phantoms...release from memories manifested as lumps of pain.

You see, the barbed wire fence had prevented my friend from escaping the enemy, tangling up his uniform and gear two feet off the ground immediately behind him. Each time I tried to pull my crouching friend free from the tethered barbed wire, I heard the screams of agony as the spiked metal tore away at his flesh. The enemy approached--a tiny black speck in the corner of my left eye. My friend was going to be left behind, captured, tortured, and killed. The barbed wire held him fast and that's when I chose to put a bullet in my friend's head to stop the suffering before it could start. I executed the shot and then ran, getting in two more rounds behind me for good measure. I had euthanized my friend in the face of terror and the point of no return kept skipping like scratched vinyl.

The cold snow from the windowsill under my tightening grip brought me back to the apartment and the horrors of surviving yet another night. Then, I made a commitment. I let myself fall. I fell backward out the open window, back and shoulders first...down...down...into the cold of night. I continued falling, letting my mind fly over the corpses beneath just for a moment...a moment long enough for me to awaken...within a mesh of barbed wire. I looked into my own face, the friendly face of mercy and shot myself-- again, and again, and again. Only to realize the terrible duality, that the man who pulled the trigger was also the man left behind. I woke up to the familiar knocking at the door, only to complete the cycle of war and come home to my own insanity yet again…

"Who is it?" I asked, knowing the answer.

Death on Wall Street

All Steven had as leverage was the truth. It had to be worth something.

The accountant licked the stamp and mailed his phone bill. He was probably the last person in the country who still used the postal service to pay his bills. Everything was digital now. There was no need for contact with the public in most business transactions these days. He liked to consider himself old school.

He didn't want to go to the party, but he had promised himself. He had promised that he wouldn't die alone. Those he admired always passed away around those loved ones they cherished, surrounded by family and friends. He had a lot of catching up to do, especially in the friend department. His friends were all virtual, on social networks and computer screens. This was the first real in person party he had been invited to since the beginning of the virus and the social distancing mandate had been lifted. He was excited, but at the same time, apprehensive. The only thing that was consoling was that he could take his phone with him if he needed to text a virtual friend in an awkward moment of social ineptness in which no connection was made and the face-to-face conversations could serve no purpose. He didn't like standing around looking stupid. He could do that at home.

The three-story brownstone was in a gentrified area of the city, a previously urban area that had been bought by corporations and reworked into condominium units for young, single people living the dream with their consumer lifestyles. The sun had just set, and the taxi driver let him off in front of his boss's brownstone with the first-floor windows bright with the activity of people already drinking cocktails in front of an electric fireplace. It had just started to snow, being the middle of December and Steven paid the driver with a substantial tip, saying, "Christmas is on me this year, man…thanks for the lift."

The car drove away, leaving Steven standing before the brownstone with the snow falling down like confetti from a ghostly parade for no one. He stood still and had the momentary feeling of the Earth turning on its axis and his body floating slightly upward. He stepped forward and the sensation ceased. He jogged quickly up the stairs and rang the doorbell.

"Steven!" a young man in a gray suit and tie shouted upon opening the door. "I didn't recognize you without your mask on…it's been a while, hasn't it my friend?"

Steven was immediately pleased with himself because he also came wearing a gray suit and a tie. He would fit in. He had made the right choice.

"Hi, Mr. Corsen!" Steven said to the president of the company. "You are looking great, sir. I am thrilled to be here, to say the least."

The two men briefly engaged in a mechanical shoulder hug, each man taking the other's hand and shaking it rapidly. They parted stiffly and both smiled at each other with expressions that reminded Steven of two disembodied, identical emojis bobbing awkwardly in mid-air like yellow floating balloons. Then both of the smiles on the men's faces faded into oblivion and their expressions turned back into mild resignation. Happy people, indeed.

Mr. Corsen led Steven into the main living room where about two dozen of his co-workers were engaged in quiet conversation, hushed tones filling the room, so it sounded to Steven like water going over stones in a brook. A babbling brook, he thought. He often saw himself alone in a field without people, without buildings or houses, but with an expansive sky overhead in which there was a burning, scorching sun that wouldn't turn off. Each waking moment for Steven he could hear the people and machines around him saying, "We have ways of making you talk…" So, he concluded he had better behave properly. Monkey see, monkey do.

"We have drinks," Mr. Corsen started. "We have food. We have pretty women. We have cigars. So, my boy, celebrate our gains tonight, for tomorrow, we go back to our masks."

Steven laughed and gave Mr. Corsen a jovial pat on the shoulder before heading over to the corner of the room to start making his way around the circus. They were all there. The CEO, the board members, the president, the secretaries and the office cogs, the paper pushers, and the number crunchers. They didn't have their masks and they all looked quite unfamiliar, especially with the bodies throwing him off, the legs and arms. He was used to talking to the heads and shoulders of people, not navigating through a sea of moving objects once again in enclosed, small spaces.

When Steven got to the corner of the room, he reached down for a drink and saw on an hor d'oeuvres platter, little bottles of hand disinfectant gel that the guests helped themselves to as souvenirs of an evening well spent.

Above the electric fireplace in the center of the expansive living room was a plasma TV that showed the stock market channel and the tally on the bottom of the screen while talking heads spouted the financials of the day.

"Well, well, well!" a young man approached Steven. It was the head of marketing, Douglas. "What brings you to Prince Prospero's castle, Steve? Shouldn't you be volunteering at a homeless shelter or something…" Douglas was drunk already, and he waited for Steven to say something, but Steven wouldn't concede. Steven walked away shaking his head, running with his tail between his legs with a plastic smile on his face. Douglas was an asshole. Often Steven got teased in the company for being the only one left who had a conscience. They knew he was the chink in the machinery, the outsider, the oddball who worked from home balancing the monthly accounts. The only reason they kept him was that he was brilliant with numbers, not one red cent gone unaccounted for. Not one decimal misplaced in his twenty years with the company. He oversaw the billions, the gross profits that both awed and repulsed him. That's why he had been invited tonight. That is why they wanted to also quickly get rid of him.

The virus had been a boon and everyone who had stock in the corporation was rolling in dough, so much so that many took vacations four times a year because the profit machine churned on its own and there wasn't a real need for employees to put their noses to the grindstone anymore. They were rolling in money and leisure time, abundance at the expense of disease.

Steven often wished he was on the other side of the table, not privy to all the financial ins and outs of the company. He wished he didn't know everything. The company had been committing major fraud for about six months now by instituting a scheme in which the stockholders skimmed off the top, the disinfectant gel actually being a much cheaper chemical compound bought overseas and relabeled for U.S. consumption. Steven knew for about eight months now that, in order to make the books legitimate, he had been expected to look the other way while shifting a substantial amount of decimal points. The higher ups had made a visit to his cramped, dank office and came by to "make sure everything was alright" and strongly suggested "you've got to do what you got to do, right, Steven…" For the time being, he was on their side, being a team player in defense, not knowing what to do for the duration of his career, let alone, his life.

Corsen came up behind Steven and poked him in the center of his back. Steven immediately jumped, almost having the drink he was nursing, crash to the floor. He turned around quickly relaxing himself, so he didn't seem as scared as he was.

"Steven!" Corsen rambunctiously smiled, an insincere sinister grin. "We know why you are here, after all, my boy. I heard it through the grape vine that we won't be needing your services any more…"

"Yes…very unfortunate, indeed." Steven spoke softly with his head looking down at the floor as if lost in thought. "After all," he added. "I've never been liked for my social graces, anyway…" The non-disclosure agreement had been signed years ago by him upon his initial hiring with the company. He remembered the rainy day he signed it. He felt apprehension back then. He felt something had been apocryphal about that October afternoon when the higher ups waited for him to sign as the rain poured outside the skyscraper glass windows behind the standing, hovering men. He had looked past their suited figures and thought of soldiers guarding the Berlin Wall of all things, signing his name carefully and painfully with a dry mouth and watering eyes.

Thirty years later and here he was again.

As the night drew on, the party had become louder and the chatter in the room more brash as people continued to drink.

"Dance, dance, dance!" Douglas swung on by with a drink in his hand, doing some stiff, awkward version of dancing. Steven heard vague synthesizer music being piped in from somewhere. "You look as pale as a ghost and just about as alive…pick up the pace, man!"

Suddenly Mr. Corsen came by and with one look in Douglas's direction, the dancing drunk smiled weakly and cowered back into the shadows, grabbing a hired woman for cover, and waltzing away.

"Shall we retire to the study for a little bit, Steven?" the boss man chimed in with a sleazy look of familiarity that made Steven's skin crawl. "We have some unfinished business to attend to."

Steven followed the tall scarecrow of a man, studying his boss's lanky wrists hanging from his rolled-up sleeves of an Oxford shirt and loosened tie.

Mahogany doors slid shut and Steven was now captive.

Mr. Corsen quickly went over to a desk drawer.

Steven closed his eyes and had a fleeting thought about his childhood when he worked on math problems at the age of four. He had loved numbers. Now, he wished he had been a baker or candle stick maker. He had wished the numbers hadn't made things at the company so transparent for him.

Mr. Corsen reached in the drawer and began to bring something out. Steven took a quick look and made a dash for the far side of the room near a separate entryway. He closed his eyes tighter, and his body shuttered. Suddenly, Mr. Corsen looked at Steven and smiled.

"Well, look what we have here…"

Steven's body froze. His eyes opened.

Mr. Corsen took out a silver pen and some papers.

"This is just a formality…we know you are leaving. Just sign your resignation on the line here…" Mr. Corsen pointed down. "Then here…" He turned a page. "And finally, at the end here…"

Steven let out a breath and stepped forward toward the desk.

He signed in silence. His body felt unusually calm and still. He realized there *was* security in numbers, more than he could ever know. Steven liked numbers again. He left the party, everyone dancing along with the music, grabbing at what they could in their drunken stupor. A stretch car was waiting for him…and it took him back home. Death had been closer to Steven tonight than he had ever known. Tomorrow he was free, but Death would continue to take its toll on Wall Street, with abundance.

Lady's Code

Part 1 —

The Big Bang and Boom Town

The rodents in the sewers had mutated into huge, bare, pink globs of scurrying, waddling flesh. Some, having never seen the light of day, had repeatedly passed down to their offspring the nocturnal phenotype of colorless eyes and completely hairless bodies. From a distance, as they stood up on hind legs, they resembled fat, short wrinkled skinned old men, naked and crouching as if in a frightened, despairing state of recoil.

The city had been hard on them, so they learned to swim like fish and balance on the razor's edge like circus acrobats without fear. Their world consisted of twisted, mangled passageways, dank cold tunnels dripping with urban waste. Their home of refuge and prosperity had been ingeniously improvised out of the rank and infested intestines of the city's massive churning digestive system. They lived off the accumulated toxic residue of the consuming population and thrived deep in the bowels of a dark forgotten underworld, nursing and surviving in the face of disease and festering biological chaos. Generation after generation they were born blind, and the labyrinth flourished…

The war had made the world very heavy, and it weighed down on the shoulders of many. We sometimes dreamed of a life without the war, but it was almost unimaginable because the war had gone on so long. Every show, news program, magazine and even the music on the airwaves referred to the war in some way each day, even if there were no new breakthrough inventions but only social commentary on the home front. The famous virtual people talked of the war. People on the streets talked about the war. Mothers and fathers talked about the war. Everyone was bonded by the war. It was something we all shared. The war. It brought us together.

I ended up being a clerk in a global administration watch and clock distribution center. Timepieces, along with fundamental living resources, were the only inventions that were supplied free and had a past inventory independent of world technology law and war product enterprise. To pass the time I imagined that contained within the timepieces on the shelves were souls. With each timepiece I gave away, I serviced the visitor with a new soul. When the watches from my shop were used, the visitor would fashion a new inner spirit accompanied with a new muse, newly acquired sins and talents. When the watches were slipped off, the person would assume his old identity and personal characteristics.

Some people obtained many timepieces from me; hence they had many souls to choose from to wear each day. The more talented and creative the soul, the more valuable the watch, or so I pretended. I was a spirit peddler. I was a time pusher. I was a dream investment broker. I was a guarantee for success, even during wartime. And this is how I spent my time, wearing my black button-down dress and imagining, fastidiously taking inventory of the hundreds of tiny boxes, trying to appease the appetites of the time conscientious, the day runners and night insomniacs.

In the Old Earth I would imagine that, as an agent of souls, I would get the best seats in the theaters, the best table at restaurants and as the apostle Judas I would slip in and out of nightclubs and parties with the greatest of ease. Yet, being still just a time pusher, I would get snickers from the elite entourages, the intelligentsia and those Old World whispering righteous people in the dark who took time from me but conveniently pushed it to the back of their minds.

Time dependent, my girl. Evolution hinges on the hands of my free clocks because after all, we got in free. Didn't we? Free.

I fill the sink in my small apartment with cool water and repeatedly wet my face. I must stay clean and pure for the evolution. The free administration psychotropics and nootropics are calling, waiting for my calculated ingestion. I'm a walk-in in my own life. Alien, estranged self. Sleepless. The war keeps my world technology eye staring at the commodity battlefields in the distance. Just believe in the inventions and you will know the release of freedom, you will know the wavering victory of an endless war.

At least I was on the neutral side, of the war I mean. I didn't know about tomorrow. Today Species/Tek was ahead twenty technology points and had the world's best inventors working toward the cause. I had known about Species/Tek since the day I was five and understood two scientific teams were competing in the evolution race. Forward/Com also won the hearts of many a civilian and promised breakthroughs solely for the purpose of evolving the species further into new scientific frontiers.

The soldiers who "fought" in the war had been trained early on in childhood in the hard sciences so they could enlist as workbench creators, conceiving and inventing their little buttons off to develop global weapons of discovery. Their "weapons" were cutting edge breakthroughs in material and energy technology that guaranteed team victory by fulfilling consumer demand and soaking up capital like a sponge.

So, the currency flowed and fluctuated, and every Earth citizen took sides in the trenches of the virtual battlefield by choosing what to buy from the consumer distribution centers and rewarded those government soldier engineers and physicists with showers of funds for more war "weapon" research and development. Unlike many years ago when war was based on territory and resources, on the New Earth the planet became communal, and the stakes were optimum consumer support based on the asset of intellectual property protected under globally regulated copy right and patent law.

We renamed our armies "Think Tanks", the soldiers became "The Creators," weapons became the "Inventions," bullets morphed into rapidly firing neurotransmitters and strategic land maps became blueprint designs. Generals became "Project Leaders" and metal dog tags turned into plastic security badges, mathematics and CAD replaced missiles and bombs. In our war, the casualties were never the dead, only the poor, those who couldn't afford access to the new technology.

With his head in a vice, each "Creator" fought the enemy with raw scientific imagination and did anything in his power to mutate his brain to the next higher level of intuitive evolution to invent what had never been invented before. When his brilliant spark had extinguished despite the psychotropics and hormone enhancers, he got an honorable discharge for service and was demoted to "Technician" from "Creator" and was replaced by the new breed, by the young nootropic drug ingesting "Creators" of tomorrow. Over and over. Musical chairs to keep the war going under the guise of human progress. Breakthrough one-upmanship. The Imagination War. The last war man will ever know. Fighting for evolution, selling tomorrow.

And I give away time for free because timepieces are the mechanical debris of Species/Tek and Forward/Com, instruments that fall into the category of communal human resources for functional survival, independent of patent/copyright law, the invention market and "weaponry" possibility. Like food, shelter, and clothing, they are provided free at Global Administration Distribution Centers. Although the "Creator's" inventions' strategic impact was acutely time dependent and the war depended on cutting edge "now" technology, it was time itself that never changed, never altered its face and inner springs and wheels. Time was the constant and because it's direction never changed, it was free, as free as an unlisted man's mind, as free as a child's imagination before Earth Knowledge Infonet Training and Conditioning.

Yet, they, the people, always want to know the time. Turn the clock back far enough and creation rewinds backward toward that infinitely dense and hot mass that was once your navel and the fist of the Space/Time expansion. Newton's timepiece promises a machine. Einstein's clock promises a face of mirrors. But I can see by the light of the direct noon sun that you prefer a watch with no hands, no face, a dial with no shadow. You are the new child, the absurd Buddhist paradox of the future. The devolutionist with the cosmic womb embedded in the center of your brain. Although I am a beggar with empty hat in hand, I will offer our man-made sundials like a prophet falling backward.

Part 2 —

Between The Ears

I'd like to tell you a little about our situation, of the affairs at hand. You see, the work of the industrial and information age has become almost all but obsolete. We are global citizens of a unique leisure class who earn our money by calmly biding our time swiveling in the pilot seat, fidgeting with the controls, and flipping on the automatic switch for amusement. Fine-tuning technology and servicing the distribution of the Creators' toys is our game as the unlisted and agreeable masses. We are here to evolve and consume and think to our heart's content. Something tells me, you like this arrangement. As life, you were born for nothing else. Right?

I wake up to the sweet, sharp menthol smell of the darwintonium sweepers flying overhead, filling my lungs and blood daily with the oxygenated nootropic enhancers which will continually mutate my gray cells for increased response. Like brewed caffeine, it affects my body quickly and I inhale hungrily sitting on the edge of my bed, awaiting the neurological absorption which will shake off the clumsy coordination of morning's slumber.

It is Monday and at 8:00 a.m. on the dot the self-driven goods dispatchers leave my order from the previous Friday at the receiving deck of my living unit. I walk over in robe and slippers and lifting the metal door of the hatch, routinely inspect the boxes of food, clothes, medicine, and synthetic chemicals. Everything I had requested was provided, even down to the one brown bootlace that had matched exactly the remaining one laced up my boot in my storage compartment.

I secretly wished for an error in the contents of the delivered packages, something that was not in my order, something that had slipped through the cracks of that great automated system of civilian goods distribution. On one occasion I even emptied all the bottles of my psychotropics and enhancer hormones and counted each one to check for accuracy. The number of pills contained always corresponded correctly to the number printed on the bottles. This morning was the same. Everything was painfully, impersonally in order and I was alone again with the chemicals, the machine made pressed black dresses, the canned food, altered neurotransmitters and heavily beating heart.

The holovision projected computer-generated actors into the dimensional space of my living room, and they acted out some obscure light saturated infomercial featuring the new cutting-edge inventions of Species/Tek or Forward/Com 24 hours a day at alternating equal intervals. Global regulations gave the two competing forces of the war equal exposure time in all media transmissions and Old Earth Entertainment was replaced totally by infomercials promoting the technology of the war. The war became our entertainment, and we escaped in the fluctuating victory and defeats of the evolution Olympics, of the reigning technology bought with the coins in our pockets.

Nootropic overdose was the leading cause of death in the new world, and I had to be careful with my biochemistry because so many others had miscalculated or over-estimated their coronary capacity. Each human being, besides being consumers in the war, competed with each other with the evolution and enhancement of their own minds and bodies. The road to success was to use the body any which way you could to get to the mind and excel retention, adaptation, improvisation, and knowledge application. Technology between the ears.

That's where civilization took seed and grew like an unstoppable virus, casting aside the body as just a means to an end, as an instrument used in the greater effort of pragmatic invention.

Earth Knowledge Infonet Training taught its pupils well. The very young, the adult, the old. "One school. One mind." they're fond of saying. Specialization kept integral learning down to a minimum, so each person didn't know what the other one was doing and there was general confusion and discombobulation between the many narrow areas of study. Multi-faceted learning was even discouraged by Infonet Training and new pupils were quickly encouraged to choose a highly planned course of intellectual development designed to fulfill a specific need of war "weapon" production.

The horses had their blinders, and we were a happy lot. Not one wild stallion in the bunch. Scientific thinking served its purpose well and we would specialize until there was total social disorientation and blind ignorance guise as the perpetual machine of invention and progress. No guy would ever know what the guy next to him was doing.

In our new world, intellectual property alone fuels the economy, and every new invention or applied thought is protected by Global Patent and Copyright Law executed and enforced by the Data-Keepers, those dedicated lawyers who draft contracts and rights for the Creators and their weapons and file everything away in the Global Library of the Human Mind in Old Earth Alexandria, Virginia. When the noble Data-Keepers weren't involved in war score keeping and invention right's protection, they walked the massive halls of the Library of the Human Mind as archivists and records pullers for paying civilians wanting access to the vast storage of technological knowledge.

As the upholders of human history and discovery, the Data-Keepers prided themselves on providing a noble and great service to humanity but not without a price. Gaining access to the library's treasures cost money and the amount of the fee was directly dependent on the timeliness of the information as determined by the date of the copyright or patent. The closer to the present the kind of information, the higher its applicable worth toward technological evolution and cutting-edge development, hence the higher its access price. Old or archaic information could be looked at for pennies and manuscripts or blueprints of speculative theory or invention, although highly innovative in nature, were also cheap to view because they had no direct present application within the time dependent war weaponry machine.

To expand the mind's knowledge with current, in the now data was expensive and cerebral evolution which hinged on the sharing of intellectual property had its cost so the have and have-nots were those who knew today's news and those who didn't, those who remembered yesterday's.

Having the evolutionary upper hand was valued in society above all else and there was a tension in the air and on the faces of humanity, an unstated desperation to push the outside of the envelope of neurological receptivity and absorption. Even dreams were scored with subliminal enhancing recordings designed to stimulate the sleeper's higher brain functions through linguistics, music, and recited technological writings. Sleeping under information sublimation was called Dormant Progressive Altered Eye Movement and waking up was termed Daily Information Internalization Surfacing. Those who chose to sleep in silence and dream unplugged were thought of as the uncivilized mentally challenged with low ambition for self-improvement and encouraged to supplement with more nootropics.

I was one of those under-achievers, one of those lost souls who chose to dream to the sounds of silence. Today was no exception, no day out of the ordinary in our determined strife as the devolutionists, as the quiet faceless minority among the loud, cheering pro-evolution enthusiasts of the war. It was not that I chose to take the hormones or chemical neuro-enhancers. It was a matter of dependency over the years because of the darwintonium sweepers, the nootropics in the water and food, that my neurology and biochemistry mutated to a point where I couldn't function without them. After years of the nervous system being jump-started by artificial catalysts in the environment there was no turning back or repairing worn down neuro-receptors so stronger dosages were always needed, even for simple normal motor response.

All it takes is a simple experiment to turn the key. The simplest conclusion is usually the best. I had been toying with time regression for some time now, various painstaking efforts at the reversal of the linear progression of dimensional reality. The trick was that it proved to not be linear at all and things seem to "happen" in a discontinuous frame of reference. Things existed in the perpetual present as flickering transmissions of an as of yet undetermined vast cosmic energy bank. To harness that bank and alter its behavior was the answer to time manipulation and ultimately to ignite the journey back to the point of creation and before.

Total and complete regression of existence was the Holy Grail of the devolutionists and promised the regaining of the perfect state of ultimate cosmic oneness. It also meant the end of war and the endless struggle of humans' attempt at continual imagination and knowledge regurgitation. Evolution through devolution was the way out of chaos and our innate suffering from want and altering desires. To alter no more and regress backward through the state of time will push the baby back into the womb where bliss and the true nature of the mind reside. "No Mind" is the heaven of our souls. "No Where" is the here and now of creation.

We called them mavericks, those independent thinkers who were self-taught and chose to create or invent. I guess I was one, but no one knew. The "maverick," if known to be so, had two choices in our modern technological society. She could either be recruited as a soldier of the War Teams with showers of promises or is allowed to practice solitary "evolution" independently as long as her new technology isn't applied as weaponry or introduced in the invention market and exists for self-growth and educational purposes only. If her choice is the latter, her intellectual property becomes protected under global common law and she can only disseminate her knowledge for free and everyone has access to the technology including both War Teams. Either she sells out and signs on the dotted line or her underpants are raised up the flagpole for everyone to gawk and point at.

Unfortunately, most discovered mavericks chose the sellout approach although the world embrace of the global common law option left the thinker with some dignity and out of the war completely. I was lucky. Being a rather ineffectual compliant civilian, I could operate my little laboratory quietly unobserved, giving away timepieces for free during the day as a government distribution store clerk and burning the midnight oil back in my small living unit, industriously pouring over the pile of notes from the previous night's experimental results…

In the center of my forehead burns the light of a million suns but I stand in the rain and the cold rising off the philosopher's stone chills my bones and flesh down to the very core, down to the twisted soul of the cursed duality. Mind or matter. They are one and I have chosen to dream the world backward and turn time back with a subtle gesture of the wrist and a handful of particle potential. Wham! Let's make this Cheshire cat stand on its head. How fast can you travel in the other direction? How far can you rewind Darwin's clock to smash the mirror? Who will you call yourself without the reflection? Who are we without history's looking glass?

Good-bye, mutation blues. Farewell to the nucleotide dance and our strange change carnival.

Part 3—

Newton In the Driver's Seat

Tick-tock, the mouse ran up the clock…

"People tell me I look just like a virtual actor." He whispered coyly at me from across the counter. It was supposed to be a secret we shared. I didn't understand the confidence. I also couldn't place the likeness.

"Can't you just see me in an infomercial, selling that bright new product of tomorrow?" He lifted his translucent solar veil and raised two perfectly straight eyebrows. "I think I'd be great in that current spot for Species/Tek featuring their new wind powered generator."

I nodded my head and maintained an open expression. He was a short graying red head with a buzz cut and fidgety fingers, eager to act but without direction. He was middle-aged approaching the golden years with a tension in his face that reflected he was fighting desperately against being given the go-by in life. The hyper neurons were firing in his head, and he momentarily wonders why he came here in the first place.

"A clock, perhaps?" I interjected softly to jog his thoughts back to the transaction at hand. A look of distaste flashed across his face as if I offended him by refusing the invitation for small talk.

"I'll take that one." He snapped, angrily biting his lip. His nimble finger pointed to a clock beneath the counter glass, an Old Earth wind-up clock with the orange and black round face and ears of Garfield the Cat.

I laid the antique on the counter and took out the giant store logbook. I carefully wrote down the make and inventory number of the clock on a narrow line, making sure all the information was correct and neatly entered. He became impatient.

"You know…" he arrogantly pointed out. "Your presence in this store is completely unnecessary. Why don't they just let us walk in and take what we want off the shelves? Hum?"

I looked up quizzically and slowly pushed the clock toward him.

"I guess I add the human touch," I said. "What's the fun of getting something for nothing if it's not taken from someone, right?"

"If you don't mind, I'd rather have full shelves and an unattended store." he waved.

"What, and miss discussing politics?" I calmly added.

"Well." He was noticeably annoyed and turned sharply toward the door. "Thank you kindly, young woman!" he shouted back. "Try and have a fun day with your little toys…"

As I watched him leave the store, I felt a pang of guilt at my obvious outward bitter disposition. It wasn't his fault. He wasn't to blame for my daily occupational obsolescence. In the days of the Old Earth, it was easy to direct your hostility. Like in some children's comic book there were the villains and the heroes, those who wanted to blow up the world and those who didn't. It was easy to tell them apart. Simple. Larger than life reality. There were the people in distress and the super humans with superpowers who would magically save the day armed with words of wisdom for the younger generation. Enemies were easy to recognize and hate with dark headquarters and dark capes, yet things became harder in the real world when the enemy dissolved, globalization reigned and social responsibility resided in the shortcomings of ourselves. Now we were our worst enemy and we were biting our heads off in the new Utopia, magnifying the meaning of human interaction and attributing a battling of wills in the stupid exchange of a Garfield Clock.

So, I try to repair the damage. We go backward, retracing the steps. The last and first temptation calls. Want for something resembling redemption? I pull out the sleek circular metal disk from beneath the inner counter. It buzzes and becomes active to my touch, already interacting with the dispersing entropy energy contained within the particles making up the mass of my hand and body. Upon turning the inner disk twice counterclockwise and presetting a dial, it super-luminously makes an assessment of the indicated targeted area and takes hold of the entropy within the space and rewinds it like the recorded information on the tracks of a cosmic hard drive.

He enters my store backward. For an instant I re-experience the obscure wave of hostility. One moment. Processing. Thinking of comic books…a fun day with my little toys…

We exchange our conversation backwards, the language sounding like alien vocalizations leaving the air and returning to our throats. He re-enacted every perturbed expression and quirk of movement down to a tapping index finger and raised eyebrow. The chemicals in my brain were reversing their neurological impulses so I sensed an underlying sensation of déjà vu coupled with the added knowledge of where I had been in the future.

He returned the clock to me…more jumbled words…he receded toward the door. Instead of a breeze with the opening of the door there was the tension of sucking air on the skin of the face. Metal slamming against metal. He was now on the outside, his mind a clean slate, the situation rectified with the aid of the regression disk beneath the forward timepieces. Instantly, when the regression time had elapsed, I jumped over the counter, my boots scrambling across the thick glass top and rushed to the door, quickly turning the latch so it locked. I then swiftly clicked a switch to the side on the wall that changed the red neon sign to illuminate the words "closed" instead of "open". I saw through the Plexiglas of the door his body approach, look up, frown, and abruptly turn on a heel in another direction. I sighed with relief. Closed to the world, for the time being.

Knowledge is a sadness I carry with me. Have the endless hours of study betrayed me? It is applicable, this method of using information, to the betterment of mankind. We will thirst no more. This is my assumption.

But what if I'm wrong? What if returning to the light is also returning to the darkness?

I once fell in love with a boy when I was twelve. He had long black hair worn tight in a ponytail and Spanish almond eyes and we would ride our solar powered scooters through the sanitary lanes between the cubical State living units. The automated wheels would turn with a rapid "clicking" sound and I would try to keep up with him and his vehicle, imagining in the rhythm and motion of his wheels was the pulse of his heartbeat.

Fueled by the sunlight, we would fly down the paved blocks, me always falling behind and him laughing into the wind. Then he would stop, and I would come up beside him, smiling across at his face that beamed with mysterious mischief and a shared secret of total freedom. Yet, although with him, I was always set apart somehow, never fully a participant in the world he inhabited and cherished. There was always the tension of competition between us even though we were probably too young to realize our playfulness was a deep seeded unstated rivalry of some subconscious dimension.

The war was going on even then and we would beg our parents for our technological toy gadgets in a fever of one-upmanship, getting our gifts of invention on New Earth holidays, trying to convince each other of the superiority of our possessions. In the end, he won out and joined Species/Tek as a junior Creator when he was just eighteen and I remained behind, looking on from the outside, tinkering with space-time in my head and playing with negative and positive energy in God's garage.

He blew me off, so I chose to blow my mind. Never got that chance to hold him and tell him I was a prime specimen for our future artificial progeny genetic alterations and mutual contractual partner growth. Never got a chance to get beyond the words, beyond the conceptualization of the thing. It was the abstraction of him in my mind, the idea of him that I loved. Yet, to this day, I am saddened I never really knew him, and he never revealed himself to me, hence, releasing me from the bonds of estrangement and mystery.

Throughout my teenage years I was already beginning to tire of technological progress fueled by the wartime efforts of Species/Tek and Forward/Com and to the dismay of my engineer parents I was showing signs of social withdrawal and innate techno-phobia. "Techno-phobia" was a supposedly well- documented New Earth condition treatable and even curable with the right combinations of neurotransmitter enhancers and daily nootropic designer cocktail. Supposedly after chemically conditioned behavior, you became a regular war hawk and vehemently bought up all the product inventions of your chosen wartime team. Through the miracle of hormone enhancement, you learned to help yourself and support the wartime effort at the same time.

Unfortunately, against my parents' wishes, I chose early on in my womanhood to refrain from ingesting certain altering "corrective" brain cocktails and continued to not go along with the beliefs of my fellow peers and the global status quo of invention fever. My "technophobia" was diagnosed as "chronic" and I was termed an uncooperative patient and the government pharmacists, and my mother and father for that matter, washed their hands and left me to contemplate on my own, experimenting with anti-gravity, optics, and magnetism. "You can't save the world…" my mother had said. "The world is your oyster…" my father had said. To give or to take? Neither. Eliminate the choice and go back before the desire. That was where my reasoning took me. Again, it was all a matter of time. No more haves and have-nots.

I wasn't like most adults my age in that I had never had physical intimacy with another human being. Because of the medical automation revolution, vaccines for any virus could be obtained in self-application kits over the counter through free distribution centers. The sexual casualties of yesterday no longer haunted the citizen's subconscious with fatal consequences from exchanging bodily fluids. Our plasma was now forever clean, saturated with the miracle drugs of the future.

Yet, I could never bring myself into the reality of that strange underworld of the great merge, the great fusion of that carnal energy of the male and female. I knew it involved a frantic mess of groping arms and legs, hungry mouths, fingers, and eyes. It was not an exact science by far. A hit and miss effort of temporary orgiastic states. Ending only in the anticipation of another try.

Many, not having the option of partnership, had many imaginative alternatives—skintight fiber optic pleasure suits, sexual hormone inducing injections, virtual interaction, brain pleasure zone electrodes, disposable self-applied brain implantation kits. The possibilities were endless. On the New Earth, the government took a very enthusiastic, passionately pro-sex stance because, after all, what is stimulation but the ultimate mind fuck, melting your face against the mirror, inducing further "evolution" and learning enhancement.

Sex was the opportunity to absorb more information. Orgiastic states were scientifically proven to encourage mental expansion and everything the government supported was for the benefit of higher levels of consciousness, altered or otherwise. Sex could be used just like drugs with cheaper replenishing qualities and all psycho-affective activities were good.

The possibility of pregnancy had been non-existent for half a century because of the unfortunate depletion of any effectual male sperm count and targeted mothers were forced to opt for the artificial egg/sperm merge under highly regulated laboratory conditions. Because of the high ingestion rate of hormones, psychotropics and synthetics, the level of estrogen and testosterone is steadily dropping in the average citizen's biochemistry so that for most, hormone therapy is a small inclusion in their daily pharmaceutical diet.

Despite designer synthetics, supplements and immunity boosters, the general over-all human physique was slowly but gradually deteriorating so that yearly there was an increase in the ante of all these miracle daily allowances that were supposed to keep us so healthy in our evolution. The saturation effect was a killer, to be sure. Sexual activity was at a high but sexual reproduction was a very hit and miss situation which depended completely on those faceless men in white lab coats with petri-dishes, incubation tubes, and genetic genome alteration intentions. Life is never enough. We always have to fuck with it.

I was a little unhinged when, on the verge of the final completion of my time regression machine and my ignition of the great cosmic contraction, a strange male came into the clock store one very sunny snowy afternoon. What was "strange" about this male human was his dress and hair. I remember obtaining a hard copy reference from my biological mother, an Old Earth yellowing book with the picture of a 19th century Victorian man with similar attire. Today we wear thermal/solar clothes made of synthetics and plastics that are usually all black or all white and our hair is traditionally short.

He had very light auburn hair slicked back neatly on all sides that stressed a perfect part to the right side of his head. Draped over his firm but small body was a long gray coat that came down to his ankles and slightly flared out at the hips. It maybe had twenty small silver buttons down the front from closed collar down to the chins and had loose militaristic style flaps over the breasts. He also wore snug gray gloves over long fingers and low heeled high tight boots that also had those strange little buttons. I was already imagining what timepiece to suggest he take and what new soul that choice would ultimately embody for him. However, the minute he walked through the door and made his way across the black and white tiles toward the counter, I sensed something was wrong, not quite right in my perception of the world.

For some reason, he looked reproachfully at me, and I inexplicably responded by flashing him a guilty glance as if I was the cat that ate the canary.

"Hellooo," he hummed, leaning his arms on the counter.

"Can I help you?" I asked sternly.

"No." he sighed and quickly laughed to himself. He put his gloved hand gently to his mouth and tilted his head as if he forgot something. His eyes searched calmly over my face, and I stood there with my heart beating heavier and sweat pouring from my forehead.

"On my way to work," he began. "I see you in here every day and you look so sad. So, I thought I'd bring you something."

I waited in horror, with an unexpected feeling of mortification. What the hell was this?

He reached somewhere in the folds of his coat and produced what looked to be some kind of flower.

"Here." he insisted, pushing it towards me.

"What…" I mumbled, unsure of what it was.

"It's a rose." he clarified.

"Oh…" I said uncomfortably, taking it from him and putting it closer to my face to inspect it. I still didn't know exactly what to do but I began nodding my head.

"Thank you." I finally said smiling cryptically and painfully looking into his brown eyes.

"Well…" he tiredly remarked, pulling up his gloves and looking down from my eyes to my chest. "Time to get back to work." He turned to go and then swerved back in my direction. "Oh, by the way, what time do you have?" he asked with a corner of his mouth turned up in half a grin.

I started as if awoken from an all-encompassing stillness. I pointed to a clock on the wall.

"There." I pointed obviously.

"No." He put a hand up. "What time do "you" have?" A finger gestured toward me.

I reluctantly looked at my own watch and told him, my eyebrows raised quizzically.

"I have 12:00 P.M. exactly."

He nodded his head and turned to go. Before he could get through the door, I asked him something in my confusion.

"…where do you work?" I asked, my voice betraying an undercurrent of strained panic.

He turned and momentarily stood still.

"I'm a Data-Keeper at the Global Library of The Human Mind."

And with that he was gone.

I looked at the rose and wondered where it came from in the dead of winter. I didn't give any timepieces to this customer, only the correct time I had. Was that all he wanted, or was there something more?

Part 4—

The Opposite Attraction of Falling Bodies

Are you awake? You sense the self slipping out to sea. And all the questions you had about this life on this spinning blue marble in space dissolve and purpose takes its thorn out of your side and you know there is nothing to know. It is not a living unit with four walls and space age windows but a strange and alien church of the soul with the help of chemical intoxication and self-induced sensory autism.

You float in your mental isolation tank and discover that collective underworld of hallucination that all good evolving pilots partake in. You're a navigator and nothing could be better in this expanding corner of the world. And just when you thought that the rubber-band physics of the universe were fathomable and operating in elastic perfection, something deep in the vice of your brain snaps and the bridge is cut forever, splitting the face of creation and destruction in two. The big cosmic freeze seems inevitable and birth and death tumble away from each other creating this cosmic abortion known as time. So, you turn up the heat so as to not feel the chill and imagine the umbilical cord was never snipped, and there is a way to get back, a way to mutate the mind and distort the soul against the reflective silver glass to awaken to that immaculate conception of astrophysics nirvana.

But the drugs in the blood are thinning and the self comes back like a boat washing up on the shore. My eyes start to focus on the ceiling, regaining their dimensional perception and I am again the lone survivor of these nightly ritual experiments. I slowly push my torso up with my arms and stare down at my stretched out feet. They seem miles away and I wonder in amazement if they in fact belong to me and actually do serve their locomotion purpose. I wiggle my toes and decide they in fact do and reach down to rub them. They have that characteristic numbness that is caused by the brand of synthetic acid derivative that remains at my bedside. Very safe but it takes a while for the blood to regain normal circulation in the extremities.

A cup of hot black coffee in the kitchen helps to bring the senses back in to this world despite my physiological cravings to remain hallucinatory and visually orgiastic. It is a little after 6:30 in the evening and I have an appointment to keep at 7:30 even though I am a little more than reluctant to go through with it. What the hell was I doing? I wasn't following my code of ambivalent detachment, but something told me lately things didn't seem to be what they appeared.

For maybe the first time in my life I got ready nervously yet meticulously, ceremoniously washing, pruning, combing back my short black hair and covering my tall lanky frame with my best black high collar street uniform. Did I look like a devolutionist? Could anyone tell? Did I betray my anger in the stoic gaze of those deep brown eyes? Ironically, I went to my bedside table and took out a watch I had with no face and strapped it vigorously to my wrist. When I looked down my hands were shaking and I stopped to relax, confused about the foreboding and angry emotions surging through me without reason. It was just an innocent meeting. I would be home in no time, both spiritually and realistically. This was inconsequential. But maybe I hear what I want to hear, my heartbeat. And it beat so heavily, with a fear and sadness I had never known before.

Out on the street, between the endless landscape of identical living units, strange humans were out sitting on their solar generators cheering and jovially patting each others' backs.   There had been a big victory for Species/Tek and they were ahead on the technology points now.   The victors sat outside their homes participating in a communal celebration, drinking multicolored brain brews, and blowing and waving noisemakers.

The sun had set, and I made my way through the angular shadows and yellow illuminated corners of immaculate artificial light and avoided the crowds of happy people and tried to leave the haunting exaggerated sounds of boisterous human achievement behind me.   Like a stream following through to the ocean, I silently and coolly walked with a rapid gait, refusing to become entangled in the blind faith of history, dismissing the war over my shoulder like yesterday's ghost.

I checked the time to make sure I wasn't late and looking down realized that my watch had no face. Great! All the buildings on the flat landscape looked the same, only distinguishable by small numbers above doorways, no signs or neon like on Old Earth.   Then evening fell down hard around me, and I realized I was momentarily lost and this meeting had become very important so I rested a minute against a living unit and watched crowds of people pass. Then I looked up to the sky and blinked hard and saw the faint pinpoint glow of a distant orbiting satellite crawl across the heavens then disappear. A pang of loneliness gripped my heart and I realized I was not only lost but also late and I wanted to return home.

So, I turned around and started to make my way through the crowd once again, damning the concrete cubical architecture for looking so similar and disgustingly uniform. Then, in the corner of my eye something remained strangely still and unmoving and caught my attention making me turn my head. Right there! Across the street waiting in a doorway was the person I was seeking to meet. He casually waved a hand at me in his long gray button-down coat, and I stopped in my tracks with a chill running down my spine. I flashed a bewildered smile, turned on my heel and tried to suppress my temptation to run toward him. Instead, I tried to casually wave a hand back and walk calmly in the direction of the brain juice bar like I had intended to do it all along. When I jotted up the steps, he gave me a long lashed wink and I had the bizarre sensation of both fear and attraction that left me totally perplexed and a little disoriented.

"You're late." he smiled, walking into the green glowing interior of the bar. "I thought you might have been swept up in the festivities of Species/Tek's recent victory…"

I laughed foolishly like a nervous young girl but said nothing to divulge my total loathing of the whole fiasco.

"It is a little overwhelming." I finally choked. "This whole war business definitely gets people involved."

He just smiled. As we approached a table, and I watched his back I sensed an eerie unstated understanding that underscored our sparse conversation. It was as if we somehow knew the score before the fact and talking was just polite protocol tinged with a strong dose of irony. Bitter pills are always the sweetest.

Before he sat down, he peeled off his constricting long coat and revealed the militaristic black robe and starched white collar and embroidered cloth chest plate of the Data-Keeper profession. As I took off my hip length drab black plastic coat, I watched him carefully pull the gray gloves from his hands and flex his thin fingers. I pictured those graceful digits touching the pages of hundreds of blueprints, documents, and patents, running those sensitive fingertips over exacted pencil marks and diagrams, protecting the world's total cerebral integrity beneath those small pale palms.

We selected our brain juice drinks from the tabletop automat console and they elevated from the servicer beneath a minute later. We awkwardly sat silent for a moment then reached for our drinks, immediately placing them to our lips. From the apparent muddy consistency and brown color of his drink I knew he chose a very strong, saturated concoction which was a mark of someone who was highly advanced in the substance ingestion game and his tolerance level for neurological arousal was probably extra-ordinary. My drink, on the other hand, was a mild inducer transparent when held to the light and smelled pleasantly of green tea instead of formaldehyde that burnt the nostrils when sniffed.

After his first gulp he tilted his head back and waited for the almost instantaneous hormonal kick, and after a slight flutter of his left eyelid it faithfully spread throughout the body, and he straightened his head and looked at me dead on. A long glance between each other heightened our discomfort and then he abruptly clinked his glass against my upraised drink and took another thirsty gulp. I resorted to monkey see monkey do and did the same while keeping a keen watch on his closed eyes over the rim of my glass.

Those eyes were the most enchanting I had ever seen in a human being, but the chiseled features reflected an inner character of secrecy and severe exactitude. It was as if I were looking into a crystal-clear pond but no matter how hard I looked I couldn't see a discernible bottom. The openness of the soul was there but its substance was disturbingly beyond any grasp of understanding so that by looking at him I only saw my own sad ignorance. In my nervousness, I fumbled in my uniform breast pocket and took out an herbal smoke, hesitantly raising it to my lips with eyes down and lit it. Then, monitoring my outward behavior carefully, I casually waved a cigarette and two fingers at his white collar and chest plate.

"Hum…" I started, playing it cool. "Are those some kind of serpents?" I asked referring to the machine embroidered design running down neatly over his chest. "I must say, it's very beautiful but I'm wondering if there is a method to the madness?"

"Oh." He looked down, gently running a calculated hand over the starched black and white design. "If you look carefully." he said pointing a finger up and down black outstretched tentacles. "You can see the reaching branches and trunk of two entangled trees sprouting from Earth to sky. See?" He proceeded to trace the body of each tree with his finger to illustrate his point. "They stand for the two pillars upon which the faith of the Data-Keeper profession rests. The mind and law as one providing the foundation for progress."

I cocked my head to one side and raised my eyebrows coyly at him.

"You know," I baited gently. "They still look like serpents to me." I took a puff of Ginseng and zoma leaf and reservedly blew the smoke to the side.

"Well…" he thought for a moment. "To some it may seem that within the sinuous branches, when the eyes stare and start playing tricks, that a serpent of some sort may appear, winding this way and that, but upon closer inspection one realizes that it's just the tree that has stood there all along…"

Hot frustration began to surge through me, and I hungrily took a sip of my brain juice hoping it would calm the rising adrenaline.

"I guess it's just a matter of time." I said, my voice unexpectedly cracking. I tried hard to force a smile, but it came out a painful wince as if my drink were too bitter.

He glanced at me and exhaled a long trembling sigh.

"In your case, it's a matter of working at that store of yours. Biding your time can be a crime depending on where your head's at. It's strange that you choose to whittle away your life giving time to others, hum?"

"I like my job," I said, defending myself. "It's quiet and people always come in needing what I may have to offer them. I have always been fascinated with clocks of all sorts and can even explain the motion of the most complex mechanics of any timepiece if asked. Even as a young girl I made my own clocks and tinkered with the gears and wheels of a rather old invention."

"You're obviously still very young." he pointed out. "Have you ever thought of applying your knowledge resourcefully in the interest of war weaponry technology?"

"No." I snapped. I thought quickly. "I'm much more satisfied sitting along the sidelines and cheering on those marvelous Creators with their magnificent flying machines. The gifted will have to do the fighting for us, and I can just as resourcefully support the cause with my discriminatory consumerism and product choices."

He looked down and smiled, obviously not convinced with my forced attempt at sincerity.

"You are very right, dear lady." he agreed in a deadpan voice. "I commend you for your support for the evolution politics of our situation. It's good to see a woman with such strong devotion and levelheadedness for the priorities at hand…"

A long pause.

Despite the stilted, reserved path of conversation, it was painfully apparent where we stood. I had maverick written all over me and as a representative of the Global Library of The Human Mind, the very serious, well-intentioned global superpower, this man was destined to hurtle a wrench in my machinery so that I could not set the coordinates of the regression disk as easily and I began to wrestle with the beliefs of everything I held true. The consensus for the evolutionists was "For now, everybody walk! About-face, sonofabitches! Forward march!" Was I so wrong to want a ceasefire? Was I so wrong to want peacetime for that battlefield of the human mind? I was determined to "think" not.

Part 5—

A Few Scattered Gray Hares

After my meeting with Data-Keeper #126, I routinely awoke the next morning to the sharp smell of the darwintonium sweepers humming by overhead. I was getting jolting shots of pain down my arm and my chest felt tight as if thirty pounds were pressing down on it. I didn't want the manual medical technicians waltzing in and shouting down at me, "Do you want your buttons?!" before tearing open my shirt and adhering those infamous purposeful bio-sensors to my chest. So, I took my fist and pounded hard my internal clock to alleviate the pain and promote some functional level of circulation. I bent over on the edge of my bed and felt the tightness spread to my neck and left side of my face. What a gas! This body better not give out on me now. Fucking piece of shit!

I stood up and regrettably felt the full force of gravity pull down on my tired body like some poltergeist tugging from the underworld. Gravity! What a bitch! I slowly forced my muscles to work and like some hung over chemical zombie, I shuffled to the living room and kitchen and selected a vitamin protein shake from my home automat. Sitting on a stool, I drank the God-awful abomination and felt over my face. Surprisingly it felt very dry like all possible porous moisture had been sucked from it overnight and left me with a reptilian leathery mask. When I ran a hand through my short hair it felt unusually coarse and brittle and to my quiet shock, little strands of it came off on my fingers, falling into my tan colored drink.

Immediately my mind ran through all the past week's ingested inventory, and I tried to attribute some cause and effect which would explain these annoying deteriorating symptoms. Frankly, it could be anything. The pharmacopoeia possibilities were too vast to narrow down. I picked out the hair strands floating in my breakfast and finished, staring at a beam of winter sunlight streaming out of the little square window cut out of the far wall of the kitchen.

In my sleepy morning contemplation, I glanced down at my hands and noticed they were somehow different as if the skin were tighter and the blue veins were more visible and raised. I momentarily put my glass down and stretched them out palms down, trying to make sure that their appearance wasn't the result of acid hallucinatory residue from the night before. You could never be sure with those tricky neurons and optical nerves. Whatever! I laughed angrily to myself, rigidly shaking off my discomfort and picking up my glass with those strange alien hands.

They were coming. The soldiers of the future, wearing their white collars and chest plates, marching through the streets in their button-down coats in perfect unison, advancing under the cause of "MIND AND LAW" to crush me beneath the great wheel. The paranoia was unbelievable and taking barbiturates was my little way of making sure that my own brain soldiers didn't advance against "me". There was a deep seeded feeling in me that was convinced Little Mr. Data-Keeper #126 knew exactly what the score was, and I prepared myself for that knock on my door which signaled the interests of outside forces concerned with the welfare of this little evolution charade. As far as mavericks were involved, the human species parade used the soft sell to lure the poor sonofabitches into the services of the war. Fascism, besides being politically incorrect, made the natives restless and giving the people the illusion of choice and free will was a hell of a crowd pleaser and mass opiate. My fear was probably unwarranted because the holy

visitation of the Data-Keepers would be humanistically, subliminally fascistic, conveyed by a warm handshake, knowing smile and showers of copyright benefit potential. "We're here to help you learn to help yourself." The old saying went. Mind warping bullshit.

The white winter light through the window crept across the floor and I finished that breakfast of champions. Gathering myself up off the stool in black pajamas that were suddenly too loose and seemed to reveal malnutrition, I went to the bathroom to prepare and suit up for the day. It was there that I discovered a new development in my senseless blind journey and stared at the mirror in amazement.

I was not the woman I was the night before. Suddenly the hand of old age had brushed across my features leaving the instant hard characteristics of a woman fifteen years older. I was horrified. My hair had gone overnight from a thick raven black to a thinning salt and pepper. My eyebrows had gray hairs intertwined within the thick dark brown strands and they were also thinner and more arched giving the eyes a forlorn appearance of weariness. Under my eyes, where there was once tight olive young skin, emerged two pale crescents which were slightly puffy from underneath and around the eyes appeared fine branching out crow's feet. The filled-out fleshiness of the features was gone leaving my face a washed-out ensemble of tightened skin, sharp angles, rigid jaw, and furrowed brow. There were even newly formed wrinkles in my long neck and my shoulders seemed bonier and more protruded severely up from under my silk sleep blouse.

Had I been stricken with some sort of overnight aging disease? What the hell happened to me? My hands were feeling senselessly over the mirror as if trying to peel back a layer of illusion. My hands dropped and fell to my sides. Well! I then let my loose clothes fall to the white tile and examined this naked specimen of sudden physiological deterioration. Let's see. Loose skin, loss of muscle tone, protruding veins, deep wrinkles, blotches of uneven pigment, tightened tissue around the bones. Definitely some kind of rapid aging. Nothing viral or bacterial I could pinpoint…

Could time have somehow accelerated internally without me externally becoming aware of it? I was sure of what day it was. It was the day after yesterday, today! Then, while stepping into the shower resigned to this new predicament, it became very clear that this was an assault on my eventual plans for the total regression and it had been perpetrated by those very protectors of the

Global Library of The Human Mind who stood for everything I was against.

As normal I went to work at the store and gave timepieces away for free to those punctually minded people. The day went by surprisingly fast, and I prided myself on not turning the key on this whole cosmic shindig and sticking around for some mutation blues fun. There it was, under the counter, the great time regression metal disk that I fashioned out of my own two eager hands, waiting for me to set the dial on the infinite coordinates and set the whole expiring energy entropy system going backward. And I could do it too! Don't think I won't! But let's see what this mysterious gentleman has in store for me with his warped Utopia of Mind and Law and all that other expansion shit. After all, the devolutionists are a force to be reckoned with, with our stoic ascetic information regurgitation and unstained pure minds of oblivion!

After work, I closed up shop and headed out into the cold for a little social gathering. I displayed my new middle-aged appearance to all the passers-by to see, tightening my dress coat around my thinning body like a shroud of newly acquired strength and honor. Fuck it all. I'm on a mission. I am immune to your absorption of me. Move out of the way. Coming through. Darkness again. Some cubicle within the maze of concrete blocks of a future civilization. I go through the door without a number or sign, and I am there. Home for the mavericks and backward misfits.

Leo Simmons. John Block. Jason McHugh. Dorothy Tyler. Brian Freely. Lisa Cabot. Mr. And Mrs. Richmond. Bill. Andrew. Shawn. Daniel…and many others, some faces I knew, some I didn't. A good crowd. John comes up to me and gives me a sideways embrace, taking my hand at the same time and firmly squeezing it. His eyes are red and tired, and they seem to be full of sentimental moisture. He hasn't seen me in a while and he's overtaken by the fact that I had bothered to show up at all, being that the war is going on so swimmingly.

"How are you, my friend?" he asks, his hand rubbing my back. He has that closed lipped smile that always seemed to underscore his perpetual reserved expression. "You look different since I saw you last, my dear. What happened? The cat dragged you in?"

"I grew old." I said, reacting with an ironic grin. "Can't you tell I look like I was sand blasted and dipped in formaldehyde?"

He laughed but didn't grasp the total truthfulness of my statement. I was serious. He chuckled away as if sharing in some sublime joke. I stared on into those gray teary eyes, perplexed.

"How's the clock business?" he went on as if tiptoeing around the mines of some substantial conversation. He always did that. Warmed up to you with asinine pleasantries knowing all too well you were there for something quite important. "How's the business of keeping time?"

I started to take off my coat and he helped, frowning his face after realizing my diminished figure.

"The clock store is doing well, John. I try not to let the little things of everyday life interfere with the big picture. Once in a while the war depresses the hell out of me. How could something that brings so many people up, make us so down? Hum?"

John took my coat and hung it on one in a row of hooks behind the door. A sad mask fell over his face, and it seemed to take all the strength he had in his small body to force that infamous thin-lipped smile.

"It's the yo-yo syndrome of society, my woman." He explained, waving a finger up and down toward the floor. "There it goes. Watch it go. Up, down, and tight and loose. One minute it's up, the next it's down and no one knows which direction is where it's "at". You know what I mean, my girl. Wrapped up in the excitement of the thing, never knowing in the end it's all wrapped up in goddamn gravity. Poor motherfuckers, right?"

I paused and hesitantly nodded my head.

"Yeah, John." I agreed. 'I know how it is…"

So, I made my way into the central living area where people sat, stood, talked, drank, and wavered drunkenly in shadowy corners. Waving hands and shaking heads. Desperate adult conversation all in the spirit of devolutionism and what this meant to a dozen and a half or so lost frustrated souls. It was a confused affair, but they had good intentions and struggled with words and ideas as if it made a matter to the world on this cold, dark winter night where the vast sky yielded only an aching loneliness. I had made it just in time for the presentations from our desperate mavericks who were fueled by the purpose of our rather ineffectual devolutionist methods.

Leo Simmons got up before the board in front of the rest of us and sketched wildly in black marker on big white paper his labored over chemical formula for a synthetic that would miraculously wean any drug saturated person off the vices of pro-evolutionary bio-chemical catalysts hence "regressing" the body back to pure form and complete unhampered sober function. He promised the concocted "flusher" would be available to all of us in injection form within a couple of weeks.

Then there was Brian Freely who spent a long-winded hour and a half revealing the research he had done in the strides of making natural laboratory independent egg fertilization possible again and naturally boosting the male sperm count to some effective level so that we could abandon the embryonic lab coats all together and regain some arbitrary chance in nature's own clever genetic "engineering".

And so, the evening went, and I sat up against a wall as still and unmovable as one of the pieces of furniture, a stoic fixture amid the painfully impersonal interior architecture of this depressing place. One by one the mavericks got up and feverishly shared their own "weapons" with their comrades and the scene unveiled comically, as if sped up in fast motion like the choppy film of some Old Earth silent movie. They gestured, wrote wildly and desperately, illustrated shapes and ideas with contorted faces and expressive hands, tried to punch a hole in that great ceiling of global progression and churning technology.

The piece d resistance of the night was the unveiling of Bill's "womb simulator X-250". He had built it painstakingly in the home workshop of his small living unit over the last year and a half and hauled it five city blocks concealed in a covered crate on wheels. We all gathered around close as he un-boxed the thing and explained the form and function of every little button and biofeedback switch.

"Welcome to the future of the past!" he said to us all with an electric smile and grand wave of his hand.

The way this regression machine worked was that you got in the fiberglass tank and laid down horizontally in the warm viscous liquid provided. Before going under the surface, you hooked up your audio feedback, inserted the oxygen tube in your mouth, plastered on the biosensors and set the desired time lapse and simulation. Then you sealed the lid and fell asleep, ready to float off into heavenly mother land. Within seconds the simulations began such as increased warming temperatures, pleasant electrical stimulation to the navel, piped in heartbeat rhythm and embryonic fluid "swooshing" sounds, and the faint murmurings of a female voice as well as complete enveloping sporadic vibrations at carefully paced intervals.

Bill suggested it was indicative to the experience to sleep on the side in a fetal position with the hands decidedly enfolded within each other. The womb simulator woke you up by a growing series of hums chanted by again, a soft female voice, and the gelatinous blanket around you became increasingly cold until you stirred from slumber, flipping the release switch, and popping the lid. Everyone clapped with teary eyes and gave Bill a good old pat on the back for a job well done.

Supposedly we were another step closer to salvation. Well!

I stumbled out into the night air, my chest tight and heavy, my head pounding with the sounds of my own blood squeezing through narrow, tired veins. It was cold and snowing and my nerves responded accordingly, gathering warm blood to the skin surface, and making my pale ashen complexion deceivingly rosy and healthy. The snow fell down heavy, and I had the momentary sensation of floating upward. My eyes fixed on the end of the street and the euphoric sensation stopped.

I wrapped the black plastic thermal lined coat around me and tried to shake off that sinking feeling of the world closing in like the cheap dilapidated sides of a cardboard box collapsing in on itself. I started walking home and casually looked behind me. Something caught my eye in the distance near the city communal square and I stopped and squinted. What the hell was that?

About a block down was a huge bulbous contraption that shimmered white metallic by the light of the moon. Upon closer inspection I made out the government printing across the metal and realized it was a darwintonium sweeper hovercraft that had crashed right there in the middle of our concrete suburban sprawl. I had heard of this happening before, but I had never actually seen the damage. Hesitantly I walked toward it and began to see the small crowd that had formed at the foot of the monstrous heap of steel, fiberglass, and rubber tubing.

It had collapsed safely enough, probably some automated malfunction that would alert mission control soon. Then as the scene grew larger in my field of vision, I saw what the "crowd" was doing. Maybe a dozen or so small children, most of them no older than eight or nine, all knelt down in the snow on their little hands and knees gathering something off the ground and putting it into their mouths. I bent down to get a closer look and saw that a blue thick liquid from both the huge vehicle's spray canisters had oozed out onto the snow making it a bright candy colored sky blue. This is what the children wanted, and they ravenously stuffed the icy chemical concoction into their faces heightening their already hopelessly stoned conditions.

I dropped to my knees and grabbed the skinny arm of a small long-haired girl, tearing her away from her frenzied consumption. She was so stoned she could barely focus on my face and the blue shit smeared her cheeks and chin. I grabbed both her arms and shook her hard, her small body and head tossing this way and that. For the first time in many years, I started to cry and pulling her hard to my chest, I let out a silent gasp of pain. I had started to rock, holding the child in my arms, and stared at the sky as if begging for a sublime mercy to release the anguish from my heart. Then she began to flail and the minute I let her go she resumed the feast with the other dazed children. I staggered to my feet and ran like a mad woman. I raced home, crying through the falling snow. "Sleep for now, children." I thought. "But tomorrow, we awake."

Part 6 —

Learning The Steps of The Dance

Again, I awoke with a heavily beating heart. Just in time to hear the sweepers buzzing overhead. I tried desperately to hold my breath but inevitably surrendered to finally inhaling my sharp vaporous nemesis. I picked up the rose that Data-Keeper #126 had given me on the bedside table and studied its petals, leaves and stem. With a feeling of confusion and subtle disturbance I became aware that its color, scent, and texture were still completely fresh and unwithered. I turned it around between my fingers and concluded that it looked strangely unreal and fake. Yet, it felt and smelled real and was of no synthetic substance. When I gently squeezed the green firm stem, it bruised so I saw it wasn't immune to the normal stimulus of the world and was in fact "a rose" in my reality.

Binary Logic

As I walked to work, the anger in me fueled a religious determination to go ahead and make that final decision to bring some kind of salvation to all the suffering souls I saw around me. After unlocking the store, I promptly re-locked the door behind me, pulled down all the metal window covers, and kept the neon sign reading "closed". Then I feverishly went to work. I was possessed with both a tremendous love and hate for humanity and damned the innate powers of pure human imagination for putting us in such a damnable place of downward spiraling.

For the better part of the morning, I systematically attacked every clock, watch and timepiece along the walls and shelves and carefully removed the hands off of every face, leaving the clocks behind up there still running but telling time for no one. This took hours and hours, but I was patient and focused on the task at hand.

As the early morning turned to afternoon, I finally finished and had accumulated a giant pile of black dials of varying sizes from all the faces. With my cupped hands, I neatly patted down on the little mountain of black, silver and gold, skinny, fat, metal, and plastic pieces. Then, placing the junk in a large metal bucket and taking a bottle of gear cleaning fluid and a match, I proceeded to saturate the pile and light it on fire.

I watched it slowly burn and sizzle as the plastic and metal deformed and congealed. I watched until the fire died down and the lack of oxygen in the surrounding air isolated the flame until it extinguished and left a rising trail of fowl smelling blue smoke. With a stiff leg, I violently kicked away the bucket and knocked the melted blob onto the floor, took the metal disk from beneath the counter and placed it firmly in front of me.

I ran my shaking fingers over the circular dials and buttons. "God forgive me." I whispered and started punching in the coordinates I had run over in my mind a million times. It was an elaborate procedure that required precision and I forced my trembling hands to carry out what had to be done. After the coordinates I had to start on the complexity of setting all the multi-purpose dials so that the entropy assessing pattern would be correct. Just as I was working on the second dial maneuver something jarred my nerves like an electric jolt that made my teeth tighten and my hands freeze an inch above the disk. A knock. A knock at the door.

"We're closed!" I shouted exasperatingly. "We're closed, forever!"

The knock persisted slow and steady.

"Come back again tomorrow!?" I yelled pleadingly almost as if it were a question.

The knock continued, persistent and patient.

I had to stop. I shouldn't have but I did.

Looking down, I splayed out my ten fingers over the disk and paused them in midair, knowing that I couldn't continue. Going to the door, I peeked beneath the metal sheet and saw that ever so familiar face, the hopeful dictator. I motioned, trying to point to the "closed" neon sign. He smiled but wouldn't go away. We momentarily stared at each other separated by the thick Plexiglas of the door. My shoulders slumped and I sheepishly put up a finger indicating for him to wait.

I placed the disk underneath in hiding, quickly grabbed my coat and keys and went back to the door. Nervously stepping out onto the street and locking the door behind me, I smiled and tried to stand up straight.

"How would you like to go for a walk?" Data-Keeper #126 suggested. "A little break from your daily routine. Some fresh air and conversation."

I was flustered and a little annoyed, but I yielded to the magnetic energy of his reoccurring presence. I resigned to the idea of him, to the ultimate meaning of him in my life that would soon be revealed. Stepping into the fire, I smiled like an idiot.

"Where to?" I asked, bowing, and stretching out a hand before him.

He held out his arm, motioning for me to take it. I did.

"Follow me and you'll see." He purred, wrapping a strong gloved hand around my upper arm.

The building was a huge geodesic dome that completely filled up the sky with sparkling steel, aluminum, and glass geometry.

"You look tired." He observed before the great arched Plexiglas doorways.

I ran a hand through my graying head of hair.

"Well, as you know," I winked knowingly. "I'm not the woman I used to be."

He tilted his head to one side and squeezed my arm.

"None of us are, you see. But then again, were we ever…?"

Above the doors was a large metal plaque with a black, stenciled embossed word across it. Just one word. Remaining up there like some obscure Zen koan:

"FORWARD…"

"Forward," he said, opening a door and gently pushing me against the back.

Through the doors and I was standing on enemy territory. The Global Library of The Human Mind. From floor to transparent ceiling, appeared the biggest interior I had ever set eyes on in my life. I stood in an expansive marble floored lobby looking up at an ascending well which led up to a giant piercing eye of the distant shining sky.

All around, 360 degrees around, on all sides of me, hugging the central well like a protective blanket were levels with balconies containing offices and industriously working people as far up as the eye could see. Periodically zooming up and down to the different levels were free floating glass transport pods carrying groups of darkly dressed Data-Keepers holding and carrying various papers, drafting tubes and white plastic file boxes. Poor legal lackey bastards.

Directly across from the doorways, several feet away from me, stood a giant statue of some sort of asexual, naked, silver painted body whose hands were outstretched toward the ceiling as if awaiting rain. On its hairless head which looked skyward and which I at first mistook wearing a crown of thorns, was a huge headdress with long extending pointed beams that were supposed to be suggestive of energized streams of sunlight. Upon stepping closer, I read the inscription under the monstrosity and registered it in my head a few times trying to achieve cohesion. It read:

"WE ARE THE COSMOS INFORMATION BANK AND WE SHALL

PRESERVE THE DATA FLOW IN OUR EVOLUTION."

I looked up again at the bald, sexless abomination, its head heavy with protruding rays, and thought what a curse it was to have such a cryptic destiny. I felt a gentle tug at my arm.

"Let me begin with the grand tour." he urged, giving me an open yet guarded glance. "Let us begin with the ground floor, the indispensable foundation of this great knowledge hierarchy."

He slid a metal card along a vertical strip and led me again through a set of massive double glass doors. Immediately, from floor to ceiling in an interior as vast as a steel paneled warehouse, I was surrounded by hundreds, thousands of thin metal drawers bearing numbers. Sprinkled amid the sprawling storage space were those darkly robed ghosts of the archive profession, opening and closing the drawers and extracting little shiny flat rectangular objects with skintight surgical gloves. They would dutifully take them to strategically placed viewing apparatuses with glowing green screens and strange metal plates for hard copy transferring purposes.

"This is building block number one." he explained. "This level houses documentation of all human invention known to exist in time and all rights of ownership, plans of construction, operation, and application. This archive area is known as the "Object

Processing Library". Here we have the majority of the weapon designs of the war and do most of our records retrieval. Everything here is stored on Tesla Hexagons and is given priority on a time sensitive basis, the most presently applicable intellectual property assigned highest demand value…"

He had long ago let go of my arm and was rigidly standing with one hand resting on his hip, thumb out, and the other cradling his chin with a finger on his temple and another seriously curled under his lower lip. By the phosphorescent glow of the bright lights, his short, usually perfectly aligned, brown strands of hair looked the most brilliant hue of strange light blue, stray wispy strands scattered oddly like sinuous branching parabolas appearing almost translucent under the white illumination.

I could smell an unusual herbal scent emanating from him when I stood close. A pleasant, slightly arousing suggestion of green leaves or freshly cut grass on an Old World Sunday morning. Yet, overriding this unusual aroma was a stronger scent of disinfectant soap, the anti-bacterial kind that fills the bathroom air after someone has taken a shower. The mixture of both these smells eluded in my confused mind a sense of retrained carnality, of a sheet of impermeable glass stretched over a sea of mud, of my eyes taking in the nakedness without being able to touch one pore of the warm skin revealing itself to me. Looking into his distracted eyes, I inhaled the smell and heavily exhaled, letting him go on with his en-wrapped explanations.

"To make things expedient," he went on leading me to a side entrance. "Let us proceed to the next level of our little labyrinth. Ignore the worker bees, they'll just distract you from the honey."

The doorway he led me to ended up being a transport pod and we began to ascend with a low, mechanical humming noise. Inside the glass elevator the phosphorescent tubing above flickered momentarily, and he and I exchanged a glance of subtle amusement. Quickly enough, the pod stopped, and a female automated voice announced, "Level Two Arrival…" The narrow doors swooshed open and we stepped out into an almost identical looking warehouse where the same anonymous black clad figures were busy extracting those precious Tesla Hexagons out of long numbered drawers.

"This is the second layer after the foundation." Data-Keeper #126 gestured, taking his hand and briefly squeezing my upper arm. "We are now viewing the "Information Processing Library". This is where we store all pertinent discoveries pertaining to knowledge such as technological progress dealing with pharmaceuticals, bio-engineering, neurology, free energy, longevity schematics, disease control and artificial food production…"

I rapidly nodded my head and quickly began to realize that the Global Library of The Human Mind had divided the whole of the human adventure solely into different expressions of mental cognition, categorized by the human "processing" of specific things. Out the corner of my eye I spotted a tall lanky black clothed figure running down one of the many extending corridors with a metal file under his arm, his shoulder length black hair falling over his face as he tried to make his way to some awaiting connection in this well-oiled machine. How very strange, indeed, I thought as if things were moving in slow motion.

"Again," he went on enthusiastically. "Everything is stored according in importance to its timeliness with the most presently applicable being in highest demand."

He smiled at me proudly, as if he were showing me the very church of man, as if he were presenting me the crown jewel hidden in the palm of his hand. He put his hands on his hips and came close.

"Do you begin to see?" he asked raising his eyebrows and looking at me sideways as if I were a shy schoolgirl learning her lesson.

Ross

I lowered my head and peered out at him, trying to figure out where the game pieces on our board lay.

"I…I…" I stammered, hesitant of opening up myself unguarded. "I'm honestly amazed at the efficiency and I never dreamed it would be this big…"

He folded his arms over his embroidered chest plate and rocked on his heels.

"The human imagination is a very big place…"

I stood motionless for a second then nervously wrung my hands and looked hopelessly around me.

"But to try to document what's in here…" I proposed, placing both my index fingers to my temples. "…is madness."

"Is it madness?" he slowly reiterated, taking his outstretched hands, and drawing them close together before him in a praying posture. "Or is it destiny? Is it just the great information flow reconfirming itself over and over again?"

Information flow…flowing forever.

I didn't answer but let his words hang in the air like a cold vapor chilling my already unhinged disposition.

Instead of delving into the deeper realm of the situation he led me to yet another echelon of the knowledge pyramid.

"Now we get into the interesting stuff." he confessed, a broad smile betraying two rows of perfectly aligned white teeth. His eyes widened and in his enthusiasm, he gently took hold of my cold fingers and raised them in a clasp as he guided us forward. "Behold our next attempt to work out the numbers and where sound meets ear, touch meets skin, and we begin to control the navigation. Level Three— "The Experiential Processing Library…"

He stepped away and turned 360 degrees around, wiggling his eyebrows at me. He then pointed up.

"Five flights above our heads reside the recorded documents of all known advanced human sentient experiments, each floor dedicated to one of the five senses. This section of our library is so vast that this level is used solely for preliminary acquisitions. Above houses the greatest leaps of intuition that the human mind has ever achieved from altered states to mental physical alteration, from long duration meditation to ultimate bio-feedback control, from subliminal consciousness to alternative scientifically tapped into realms of uncharted human reality."

He eagerly stepped toward me then quickly pulled himself back. He wanted to reel me into the boat with all the other flailing fish. I saw a look of desperation flash across his eyes then anger. Would I embrace that sacred tablet of etched human life as truth and salvation?

Would I digest the living knowledge of humanity as just "information"? Is this my ultimate sin?

I saw his graceful, gloved hand calmly stroke down against the carefully buttoned front of his concealed chest and then drop to his side in a clenched fist. His face turned strangely seductive, and fear leaked through me like flight or fight serum seeping from the primordial crevices of my brain. He came close, too close, and I felt a surprisingly calming drainage from my protective aura that I had clung to so dearly.

"Devolution is a joke…" he whispered. "Watching shadows cast by the sun leaves no time on your hands. Don't you see, no end, no beginnings, just circles…just circles…"

It was then, like a sword in one triumphant swing, that big bangs and expanding space-time was cut down to a deformed twisted creature of my dark delusion and the sequential order of things got jumbled. The numbers one through twelve failed to correspond to the position of the sun across that plastic backdrop of sky. Why? Why were the worker bees hoarding all this data in their little numbered honeycombs? Law protection for war weaponry was just the surface of a deeper mysterious ocean and I was starting to drown. It had all been misdirection, the war. But why?

With my soul free-falling, we continued to ascend through the levels of taste, touch, scent, and hearing to the last level of the Experiential Processing Library, where human experiments with sight were stored. It was there in a secluded corner, away from the bustle of information processing Data-Keepers, that we stood silent and exchanged tense looks of recognition.

I carefully slipped my trembling hands around his strong shoulders and pulled him inward, heating my chilled arms and torso with his warm body temperature. We embraced stiffly, his breath expelling near my ear, the side of my face touching his soft hair which made me think of old black and white photographs from eras gone by.

We began to rock, strangely cradling each other like two strangers who were on the verge of becoming indistinguishably close, losing ourselves in spite of the internal fight. We clasped hands, he put a hand on my shoulder, and we gradually engaged in a dance, a close-knit waltz where we turned and turned in circles…circles…a tight loop of intimacy.

"More awaits us above." he confided, his lips brushing against my tight jaw. "But I will save the best for last."

Part 7—

The Release

The white electric numbers by the bedside glowed 6:37. I stared at them for a while... 6:38...6:39...6:40...until they began to speak to me, not as numbers but as symbols of a strange electric dialect. They appeared transformed and alien as if with every passing minute there was something the digits were trying to tell me.

6:41...6:42...6:43...There was something wrong. I didn't feel like myself. I felt older. I felt I was racing with myself, and I was falling behind. A part of me was way ahead and the other part was left in the far distance.

I reached for the clock and inexplicably hit the front of it hard against the side of the night table. The front electronic plaque fell out into my hands. It dangled from the clock from two wires, and I yanked it free and turned it in my fingers. On the backside of the display tablet was a digital chip that dictated the sequence of the numbers.

I threw the thing onto the floor and carefully looked at what remained of the clock. Beneath the display unit was a glowing little screen of pure white light. I ran my hands over it and watched the flesh and blood of my fingertips become translucent. It took me a moment to realize that for as long as I could remember, I had just seen the numbers and the light beneath had eluded me. Light? Light…A strand of gray hair fell from my head and landed on the back of my hand.

Turning my head, I noticed a glass half empty with water on the nightstand. It had brown residue resting on the bottom, a nootropic concoction from the night before I had taken to help me sleep. I turned my head in the other direction. On the opposite night table were dozens of bottles containing drugs of every imaginable effect, most of which I presently took to retard my newly acquired aging process.

In front of me were holographic images of two virtual actors demonstrating the operation of a new bio-feedback monitor designed by Forward/Com. They had electrodes taped to the smooth digitally enhanced skin of their temples and foreheads that were attached to horrible wires which ran back to these black and silver oblong control panels. The synthesized actors closed their eyes in concentration and funny red, green and yellow lights on the monitoring panels responded wildly. Incidental classical music swelled and there was a glitch in the holographic transmission that made my eye twitch.

I put the broken clock down and crawled forward out of the bed and into the wavering three-dimensional infomercial. I stood there momentarily with the cold blue and reds of the laser light particles playing off my dark sleep clothes, trying to get a bird's eye view of the world I thought I had firmly pinned under my thumb.

The Data-Keepers were coming. He was coming to take my distraught face between his hands and lay my tired head down on the sweaty pillow for the last time. Like the sublime stages of R.E.M., I felt my waking life drift away in layers, each cloak of consciousness fading so my sleep became a frightening realization of a dreaded waking hour.

In utter mortification, I gawked in the bathroom mirror with my hands pulling at the tightening skin of my sunken face, my mind racing to connect the pieces of a puzzle I intuitively felt I already knew the answer to. Age forty-five, fifty? Each time I saw him, years of youth were robbed from me, and my cells died and transformed in their accelerated degeneration. Curious yet tragic. The price we pay for playing the fool.

A far corner of my living unit was occupied by a strange woman, myself. I passed my hand over the stranger's workbench, the numerous instruments of particle interaction osmosis and energy transference—the magnetic and artificial inertia generators, the hydro-electric timepiece intestines which coiled like snakes around wired veins, tiny photon fed dimension crunchers and stacks of handwritten pages containing drawings and spatial equations.

To the left, by a small welding device, was a piece of crumpled paper that I reached for and unraveled. It was a digital printout from my home Species/Tek Blood Analysis machine from several months ago. I read the long-detailed breakdown of chemicals and foreign bodies floating around in my scarcely human plasma soup and laughed, letting the paper fall to the floor.

Just then I heard the darwintonium sweepers starting their rounds overhead and almost immediately experienced the lightheadedness and delusion of immunological elevation. There was the sensation of warmth on my arm? I turned toward the open living room to witness the winter sun rising and pouring through the narrow window slots. I walked toward the windows and into the sun's rays, my bare feet following the warmth from the beams hitting the cold, sterile silicon tiles.

"Is this your first time to the window?" I faintly heard a male voice ask through the dead of air.

Micro-universes dancing in space, each pouring golden beams encompassing trillions of particles all sharing information and speaking to me in transmitting whispers of wave vibrating silence. Holding up my hand, I realized the light went through the skin and bone, yet I had a grasp of the information, I had a hold on the radiating data flow through a divine conduction. Albino, colorless and as blinding as an immaculate white laser injection into the vice of my primate mind, the light seeped into the dark core of the soul, awakening the sleeping giant within to see what was behind her.

Drunk and awed from the illumination, I slowly turned around and stared at the far wall behind me. Feeling like I had let something slip from my fingers and fall to its death, I realized I cast no shadow and saw only the square shadows from the windows themselves. A broken woman of sagging flesh and brittle bones, I held up my arms like a straw stuffed scarecrow, watching the wall for a sign of movement. Nothing. Only light and windows. Scarecrow woman.

Is this your first time to the window?

Have you been here before?

Picking up information for the next time around…circles…loops…

"It must be love." a voice said from somewhere in the room. I turned to acknowledge my hallucinogenic projection—melting neurons dripping from a liquid mirror. Relativity shows me the eternal joke.

An old man in suit, tie and waistcoat with wild, disheveled gray shoulder length hair stood on his head balancing perfectly in the middle of the room. Einstein?… A hallucination?…

"He's the apple of your eye." He winked mischievously. "I can tell it was love at first sight, tug of war with the mud between you, the push me-pull you's of the cosmic circus, poor lovers of the great galactic mind merge."

I came closer, calmly putting my hands on my hips, patiently waiting for the optic illusory episode to fade.

"Proper time is no time at all." He regrettably sighed. "…relatively speaking, of course, with the speed of light in mind." He momentarily reflected still up-side-down and wiggled his shiny brown dress shoes in the air. "Without knowing it, I lived my life up-side-down and should have inverted the principles, flip-flop, flip-flop, entrances and exits never being what they appear to the staggering actor on the stage…"

I backed away and the hallucination seeped back into the internal synaptic river, returning history's archetypes safely back into the protective subconscious.

"Albert…" I whispered sadly toward the empty space. "I would have bravely faced the end to embrace the beginning, but I didn't know the candle burned at both ends. I just assumed there was a first and last step to our little journey this time around…But it looks like the serpent is hungry for its own tail."

With this human suit, betrayed by my own skin and bones, I awaited a strange destiny that involved my fall and eventual metamorphosis from the ashes into something unreal and far removed from my previous sleeping life. I felt the tension of change in the air, the unpleasant suspense of reluctant transformation. My mind said, "no", but the heart, that big thumping rabbit scrambling down the hole said, "go like lightning."

The war. The haves and have-nots of the information shuffle. Games of withholding the brass ring. Staffs of golden snakes helping the ancients make their way down one-way roads.

I thought of Data-Keeper #126, carnal thoughts of deep seeded lust and craving, thoughts that were usually lobotomized by the internal chemical infrastructure setting up government in the fluid of my veins. But the cravings came as obvious and disturbing as a long-haired albino standing by a wire barbed fence in the black of night, just staring back at me through the pane glass of my impotent black sun soul.

So, like a zombie with the on and off switches flickering, I went back into the bedroom where the elaborate orgiastic state 2500LT machine was and began to lower my sagging pajama bottoms. It would do all the work with the miracle of automated metal fingers, pincers, gentle sponge levers and synthetic lubricant to simulate warm body fluids. Virtual sex.

The clever machine started to hum and vibrate with its own industrious pleasure and before I could prepare my tired body for an orgiastic state, I stopped. I stepped back, sighed, closed my eyes, opened them again, and blinking hard and studying the monstrous piece of shit, realized all I could see was a goddamn coffin staring back at me. Fucking technology, it'll get you every time.

My female body lies before me, stretched out naked, an effervescent, heavenly plasma sheet of sky. My eyes and lips disappear like footprints in the clouds, and I permeate rubberized planes of space and time with the elusive ether residue of a messiah's cool exhale. Delusions of cosmological constants. Fudging the numbers so the stars won't fall.

I try to fight the dehumanizing blues by opening the womb of an empty ocean with maximum thrust, throwing out my DNA creation flux like a discarded card from my hand onto the table, hoping a kingdom will flip out across the optic field among the gambling chips and coffin nails giving me a full house.

Release after release, I think of a golden immaculate cosmic contact with the impenetrable plasma hanging over my head, but the white protein serum is out there hanging off the stars, entangled and fucking with my head like some fetus neuro-implant, and he's out there using your orgiastic nirvana to spin a web with the fertile genetic shit so that my altering cosmic reflection has turned me into a fly.

My head was in my hands. They were shaking, impulses and synaptic erratic conversation. The men in the white lab coats had sterilized me and my medicine cabinet full of pills had finished off the job. Give me the power. Give me a fucking fertilized egg! I am the motherfucking egg woman! Aren't I the co-pilot on this mission or has ground control put me in the chair without any manual?

My hands were the first to go for the thing. The 2500LT machine was yanked from its plug and plummeted to the floor with a dead thud, the lack of electrical ignition ceasing its robotic seductive purring. I fell and threw myself at it, kicking it with bare feet and pulling at the artificial levers and knobs like a madwoman.

The thing was indestructible and with every blow, the skin of my fists and feet snagged and tore making my flesh a bloody mess. No more mind fucking from this piece of engineered shit. I'm on manual, you rotten soul sucking pumping kitchen appliance!

With bloody hands and feet, I picked up the metal and rubber lover and carried it toward the front door, struggling under the substantial weight of it, the fastening claws at its base digging into the torn skin of my palms. Awkwardly opening the door, I flung it with a primal grunt onto the paved concrete in front of my living unit and it fell down hard still in perfect functional condition but cracking the pavement underneath.

"Get back!" I screamed, out of breath, my teeth clenching so tightly my gums hurt. I was breathing heavily but after a few seconds I heard someone elses panting overlapping my own. I peeked around the corner of the doorway to the side of my dwelling and saw a frightening sight.

Crammed against the outside wall of my home like a Gothic creature caught in the noon sun stood a darkly clad figure hugging an armful of metal folders and half a dozen little silver square disks. His face looked tired and bewildered but there was an impish elation behind his middle-age pale blue eyes and slightly smiling parted lips. At first, I was guarded because he wore the black long robes and high white collar of a Data-Keeper but when I looked down to his uniform chest plate it was covered in blood.

"My God!" I panicked, stepping toward him, reaching out with a bloody hand. "Are you hurt!" I put both hands protectively on his shoulders, searching quickly over his chest for the source of the wound.

He was confused, then whimsically amused. He had the preserved aged appearance of all good evolutionists who belonged to the formaldehyde club. He tried to catch his breath and resting his head against the concrete wall, pensively searched toward the sky, laughing between labored puffs.

"Don't worry about this." He calmly reassured, gesturing one of his encumbered hands clumsily toward the smeared chest plate. Momentarily forgetting his bliss, he cautiously shifted his eyes in the direction of the metropolitan square. Then he looked at me with a flash of sadness. "This mark of Cain on my chest is just a splash of red acrylic paint from an air canister so we can tell each other apart. The dominoes fell from the inside out this morning at my place of work, at the Global Library of The Human Mind…"

He lowered his head and a graying strand fell over his left eye, but he peeked mischievously across at me, waiting for me to pick up on the total significance of the situation. The right corner of his mouth started curling up and with arched eyebrows, he gave me an almost seductively inviting look. Then he glanced out into the street at the marvelous 2500LT machine, and he briskly shivered as if shaking off a cold wind.

"We had a little bit of mutiny, and our beautiful cathedral has started to fall." He smiled, shoving his miscellaneous armful of shiny metal folders and flat square numbered boxes at me while keeping an eye on the activity down the street. "Welcome to Old Earth Alexandria, you lucky bastards!"

He kept shoving the stuff at me and I just stared. Behind him in the street suddenly emerged a strange sight, the surreal image of black robed figures running, first one, then two, then three and more and more, all carrying as much documents and disks as their arms could hold.

"Take it, you idiot girl!" he screamed angrily, sending a jolt to my raw survival instinct buried deep under the wiring.

I obeyed and clumsily took the offering into my arms.

"It's your baby now!" he excitedly breathed.

"What is it?" I asked, the awkward echo of the words hanging in the air as if for a second, we both thought the brief silence afterward was the answer.

His forehead furrowed and his lips trembled with a sign of relief. He was in a hurry, having just branded himself to free the ghost and toppled the bank onto the floor in one decisive swoop.

"It's free." He spoke close, a hand rapidly patting my shoulder. There were tears in his eyes. "I...I don't really know what it is because I grabbed what I could but...in general they're patents, designs, and technical documents..."

He swallowed hard and passed a stretched-out hand over the armful of information as if blessing me to take what he had given me.

"...the stuff could be thirty minutes old, twenty, thirty years old or hundreds of years old...it doesn't really matter, you see lady, as long as it's in your hands...the war can't go on because everybody knows...everybody knows, and nobody can win because there's nothing to lose..."

We looked at each other then he began to make his escape, frantically wiggling out of the robe and letting it fall to the ground, so it looked like a broken raven in the snow. He quickly turned back at me and exasperatingly ran his hand through his hair.

"Funny little tinker toy, human nature is! That one's for free!" he yelled and disappeared.

"For free…" I whispered, holding onto the treasures of Alexandria. "Free."

Part 8 —

Scattering The Peripheral Layers

The Data-Keepers with red smeared chest plates and armfuls of human history were scrambling through the city knocking on doors and surrendering their high security jobs to the strangers of mass consumption. The confused citizens came out of their confined concrete living units into the winter light and with baffled looks liberated the frenzied Keepers of the economically sensitive baggage not knowing, being themselves only children, that they had inherited the kingdom.

The streets and town square were filled with fighting, struggling black clothed figures battling over slim metal boxes and shiny folders, using their fists, feet, teeth, and nails as weapons against newly uprising enemies. Some wrestled and rolled, choked, and throttled, leaving blood in the snow in the cause of their mission to uphold or unravel the delicate balance of civilization. Because the Data-Keepers were assigned identities numerically, the fighting former co-workers addressed each other by number in their anger and the city was full of the sounds of shouting digits.

"147, you can't believe the negative consequences of your rebellious actions! Don't be rash and destroy everything we've been working for all these years…Give me the archives now and we'll go back and talk to the executive branch and work the problem!"

"Work the problem?! Fuck you, 78! I'm fully aware of the situation and our occupations aren't in the equation! Don't you understand, you impotent slave, our obsolescence is our liberation and for the first time we'll know the uncharted seas of discovery during peacetime. We can learn together! What a fucking concept! Knowledge without commodity and enterprise, driven not by the flexing muscles of greed but by the rewards of co-existence, of the great human unification!"

"147! Shut the hell up! You're out of the loop, bastard! What the hell made you think this miserable job had to do with humanity?! We're not in the best interest's business, we're the most sacrilegious meat market there is, that of imagination, caging those fluttering birds within man's soul. Imagine…we encourage and make it our jobs to take that inspired maiden and prostitute her around town."

"I'm no pimp! Not any longer!"

"Withholding information makes you an accessory to the crime, 147!"

"No more! Out of my way, 87. The bridge will be raised!"

"Pimp!"

"No more!"

"147! Give the shit back, you traitor, or I'll take it back by force…"

"Try, 87! I'm a gladiator with a mission, spineless sonofabitch and I've got hundreds of thousands of history's ghosts on my side wanting to go home. We're going home! Home, for Christ's sake!"

"Don't be part of the problem, 147."

"Eat shit, 87. You're my problem."

"That's it! Take on the big wheel, you little shit. Come on!"

"Agreed, you Nazi asshole. Becoming part of the solution, now…! What goes up must come down!"

So, the punches rolled and the documentation flew and this is the way things went in the streets of our new engineered Earth. Fighting and shouting Data-Keepers were everywhere, spitting and tearing each other's robes off, battling over files and Tesla disks, rolling around in the snow as if engaged in some symbolic Kabuki dance of mystical powers. Musical chairs. Everybody dance!

Around and around and under and over, tumbling in a desperate free-fall of man's strength and weaknesses. Trying to keep the keys of salvation, the darkness and the light, the blinding, and the awakening, out of the wrong hands. The town's people, the sleepy creatures of Earth, upon realizing what was actually going on, watched the hundreds of Data-Keepers in their havoc and cheered in awe and exhilaration.

The Keepers rebels, having the empowerment of a mission running through their veins and psyche, were strangely possessed and overthrew their opponents with unearthly superhuman strength and determination. And the illumination came to the rest of us with the passing of knowledge from one trembling hand to another, the surrender of the painful job of blinding brothers and sisters through the generations, of keeping the baby quiet so the offspring eats what's on the plate without asking any questions.

"I'm making my ultimate connection!" one rebel screamed manically, laughing like a lunatic. "This is the final judgment, laboratory conceived bastard! Out of my way, motherless fuck…"

"They must know!" another howled down at the red face of his choking victim. "No more price tags for the dreamers! The gypsy blood of night flows into the dawn, evolution fucker, so give it up…"

The gatekeepers were tired, very tired. Their occupations had weighed down so heavily on their hearts that the poor souls had been pushed to the very edges of sanity and the internal turmoil had released itself in this human circus on an otherwise unassuming sunny winter afternoon.

Then the neuro-stasis brigade landed on foot from the doors of floating hovercrafts and tried to make their way through the chaos attempting to execute the long mental stun with some kind of discrimination. They carried their polarizing neuro-stasis rods and gave unsuspecting victims a quick jolt for a long unproblematic sleep.

Yet, as the citizens progressively took the Global Library's documents into their own possession with childlike joy, things went wrong for the government passive law enforcers. Both Data-Keepers and townspeople now had the neuro-stasis rods and were using them to their advantage by immobilizing anyone who looked suspicious to their own agendas of justice.

The silver suited law enforcers were being tackled down for their brain numbing weapons and soon found themselves sleeping on the job, unable to infiltrate the uprising with any respectable efficiency. It was embarrassing. Many descending ground troops chose to refuse descent into the crowded streets below and re-closing the hovercraft doors, industriously whisked swiftly up and away into the sky back to that invisible infrastructure of mission control and command.

I started to laugh, standing in my doorway with my newly prized documents cradled in my arms like some hard-copy techno-baby wanting attention and maintenance. Still in my dark pajamas and slippers, I walked calmly through my town, avoiding the tumbling bodies, the rolling masses of robed fools grunting with curses and jerks of comical physical exertion, the flying metal disks and open flapping metal folders skipping along the ground.

Seeing a wide-eyed perplexed child pressing his body against a corner of a building for protection, I approached him and unloaded my intellectual property on him, forcing it into his little arms knowing all too well he was an innocent who would do the information well. For some reason, I did not feel the cold like I had before so painfully because the strange faces of humanity didn't seem so strange anymore. It started to snow. My feet crunched like brittle wood against the ground.

The timepiece store in which I had kept attendance and bided my time had been broken into and every single watch and clock had been stripped off the walls and shelves despite their absence of working hands. At that point, I wasn't quite sure if they knew the machines couldn't keep time or had they taken them for that very significant reason. Look, Ma! No hands!

I suddenly panicked and realized what I had carelessly left under the counter. A wave of dread paralyzed me and the fear of everything suddenly morphing backwards in a frenzy of accelerated regression raced through my mind, nightmarish images of men and women crying in pain because they had become children again, embryos, gamites, DNA in the blood stream, faces of ancestors, animals, bacteria, energy impulses giving birth to dimensional confusion…then…

I desperately ran over to the counter and searched underneath. There, wedged in the corner where I had left it was my dreadful invention, shining perfectly in its spherical functional design, waiting for me to make the choice, to take a step forward or back all in the guise of seeing the light. However, to my dazed amazement, sitting there taped to the disk's small control panel was a piece of paper that read:

"YOU'VE BEEN THROUGH THE FIVE LEVELS. THE REST OF THE ANSWER TO YOUR QUESTION LIES ABOVE…DATA-KEEPER #126."

Then at the bottom of the words was an ink stamped insignia of the image of a sun. I angrily snatched off the paper and, holding it close to my face, frowned at it, repeatedly shifting my eyes down to the little neatly stamped image, trying to keep ahead of what the hell was going on.

I was getting paranoid. Whose side was he on? Had he resigned his profession? Was he a rebel now? What color was his chest plate and who did he really want to have the information property? He had lost and his worshiped pillars of law and knowledge had crumbled. Or had he helped with the downfall? Could he be trusted? Who was rattling my fucking cage and who held the key?

With the cosmological doomsday machine under my arm, I started again out into the winter afternoon, holding onto the damn note like an imbecile knowing I should just devolve every God forsaken soul to oblivion. But I didn't and kept walking, noticing I cast no shadow against the blinding white snow on the ground and that despite the frigid air, I was getting uncomfortably warm and clammy.

Behind me I heard the faint melody of the victorious townspeople singing a song that sounded like "Row, row, row your boat" but I couldn't be quite sure. I stopped momentarily and looked straight up at that penetrating orb, that great spotlight in the sky that saturated every corner and nook of your little life with the intangible effervescent milky veil of daylight. Keep walking. Walking. Walking. Ignore the machine.

The Global Library of The Human Mind looked ravaged, the doors yanked off their steel hinges and the stairs littered with technological blueprint debris. There was a huge crowd of people waiting happily to get in and others shuffled out carrying armfuls of archives. Finally, there was something besides the war that brought them together.

As I slowly made my way through the gathering toward the inner lobby, the smiling townspeople were gently pushing me forward and strangers encouragingly squeezed my skinny arm as if silently communicating a new hope.

When finally inside, I saw Data-Keepers with red smeared chest plates faithfully guiding people around the ground and upper levels, helping the wide eyed children take home everything that was stored in those thousands of sacred long thin numbered drawers.

Directly in front of me in the lobby was the huge statue of the silver painted naked icon of the Global Library bank looking toward the sky with its crown of sunlight beams. Yet, on this monumental occasion, it had been hastily altered and hanging from the pointed beams of its crown were large pieces of thin onion skin paper going all the way around, and imprinted on these pieces of paper like children's mischief were handprints smeared in the infamous red paint. Again, I read the inscription in marble below the statue:

"WE ARE THE COSMOS INFORMATION BANK AND WE SHALL PRESERVE THE DATA FLOW IN OUR EVOLUTION."

To the side there awaited an empty transport pod with its doors patiently open. The overhead lights in the elevator flickered as if there was a wobbling power shortage, a breakage in the electric current feeding the glass womb's ghostly illumination.

With my little machine cradled in my arms feeling like I had somehow missed the starting gun, I stepped into the transport and pressed "5", hoping the pod had enough energy to power me higher. The doors closed and I was on my way, past the Object and Information Processing Levels, through to the Experiential Library. As I rose, I watched through the glass walls the havoc that unfolded on each floor, smiling a wry grin all the while knowing the pendulum of power sways with predicted precision…

Alexandria, don't forget me because I am the heart behind the hard-copy. I am the hardware behind the engineered dream of Utopia. No matter how many numbers, letters, and images flow through your gates, I am the witness. I am the gatekeeper, and nothing gets past me unless I can imagine it. Alexandria, release the ghosts in your machine. We must imagine.

EXPERIENTIAL PROCESSING LIBRARY…

LEVEL FIVE—SIGHT…

My first destination. The transport pod opened its doors on level five, and I stepped out onto the slick floor with my slippered feet. I had already surpassed the levels of sound, touch, taste, and scent. The school room was behind me. Lessons within a dream.

I immediately saw the same confused state of affairs—Data-Keepers everywhere taking the children under their wings and entrusting the townspeople with documentation of thousands of sentient human optical experiments. Then, to my elation and delight, I saw the person I wanted to see.

Data-Keeper #126 was standing in a far corner of the huge space like a frozen alien spirit with his back to the wall and his eyes on the shifting world paradigm. The hungry souls of humanity moved before him and he took it all in like an animal of prey scanning the territory, sizing down the perimeters to compute the equations.

He held up a hand to acknowledge my presence. I also held up my hand and wondered if we were saying hello or motioning the universal signal for stop.

Greetings and time-out. Hello and good-bye. I made my way across the library floor and slithered cautiously up to him. I quickly noticed that he wore his gray Victorian overcoat, and I couldn't tell if he was a rebel or which chest plate he now wore.

"Why are you here?" I asked quietly. "It's not really for the war, is it? Is there something I should know, #126?"

He slowly took hold of my shoulders and shook them gently in silence while giving me a look that I could only describe as unearthly. His eyes were full of empathy and a deep understanding for me. I became frightened and for once in my life I put my fate in this man's hands. I let my head fall and felt a heaviness lift from my heart.

"Who are you?!" I asked in eager desperation, trying to keep myself together.

He took my head in his slender hands and raised my face toward his so I could look into those open eyes of Heaven's gates.

"The question, my old woman, is who are you?" he sighed. "Who are you in the light?"

Part 9—

The Noonday Transference

Into the transport pod and ascending….

"The levels below, dealing with the storage of information, object and sentient human processing are quite unimportant to our real intentions." he explained, taking some sort of bio-sensor and scanning it over my body. "Alexandria's lower levels exist as a kind of pleasant diversion for the civilized mind. A kind of detour before the road less traveled. As you can see, there are many levels above the Experiential Processing Library of Sight, yet most don't ask questions because the lower archives keep humans busy with information absorption purpose."

He took the small bio-sensor and began pressing its buttons and checking its little display screen.

"Hundreds of years ago during Old Earth operations we erroneously built various receivers designed to pick up on signals transmitted from extraterrestrial intelligence, mistakenly thinking the alien signals of communication would exactly correspond to our engineered receivers. We also erroneously believed that these signals would originate from organic biological entities similar in physical DNA although different in appearance and structure.

"Yet, about a hundred years ago, a mathematician by the name of Dr. Edith Wyman, working with the extraterrestrial interface program and using her own mathematical formula, came across repeated mathematical constructs contained in her analysis of electromagnetism and the wave patterns of light. After further analysis over a twenty-year period Dr. Wyman and the E.T. interface program realized that her mathematical constructs revealed a highly complex ongoing text of encrypted communication and the transmitted signals we were trying to receive with our equipment were not organic in origin but were being sent to us in the very energy frequencies of light waves. The close encounter we had been waiting for was not in the structured form of matter but had manifested itself as a tensional force of the universe...The light itself contained a highly complex conversation…Light itself is the E.T. signal…"

Data-Keeper #126 paused and whisked a small communicator from the folds of his heavy high collared coat.

"Phil, this is Noah." He spoke rapidly. It was the first time I had heard names associated with actual people of the Data-Keeper profession. His name was Noah. "We are ascending on our way now. I have the connection with me. She seems a bit lost but in perfect reception condition."

He looked over at me and reached out and pinched my chin with two of his fingers.

"How are you feeling?" he asked me while still on the teletalk.

"Like a million dollars…" I replied flatly staring at him. Dollars and cents had gone out with Old Earth economics, and I said the phrase to emphasize my total feelings of obsolescence.

"She's doing just fine." He said into the flat metal mouthpiece to Phil. "She may be lost but she's definitely kept her hat on at the crossroads." Noah paused and glanced at an instrument around his wrist. "Arrival in forty secs, see you in a bit for confirmation, Phil."

With that the communicator disappeared in those Victorian folds and he smiled a huge, joyful smile, a smile I had only seen as a child when I happened to catch myself in the mirror. Hey, that's me…and I laughed…and laughed…like now.

Laughing. We had both come to the right place and every place was interchangeable, spinning, tumbling, a passing panorama of sentient illusion where we met at the crossroads and kissed. Laughing.

"The levels we are ascending through," he beamed. "are the pinnacle of our relentless archive maintenance. Beyond Experiential Level Five there is nothing but light assessment and analysis based on Dr. Edith Wyman's work. Dozens of levels dedicated to experimentation, usage, observation, convertability and encoding of transmitted light…"

"Transmitted?" I repeated, my eyebrows arched, my body aching from aging muscle fatigue.

"Yes!" Noah almost shouted in his brimming enthusiasm. "We've translated specific patterns of frequency associated with wave theory and painstakingly, with the help of Dr. Wyman's documented mathematical systemic analysis, paired it together with human neuropathways mapping linguistic function. The light which has been the source of life for everything in the Earth's bio-sphere has not only been helping life to bloom but has been simultaneously transmitting vital information to us and all living things in this perpetual process. We are the physical manifestation of the transmitted signal, the functional translation of the light's data. We carry the message with us. Until Dr. Wyman and solar-metrics, we had been too blind to realize it and instead built our radio E.T. interface transceivers and completely overlooked the great information plasma oozing everywhere around us. God's plasma! The great omnipresent telelines of divine communication! Light!"

Numbers reveal the dance. A circle of angels dancing around the origin of zero. Numbers in the mind of a woman. Numbers as the shimmering faces of our gods.

The transport glass doors opened, and I was hit by the direct sun pouring down on me from the hundreds of triangular windows making up the ceiling of the geo-dome. We were walking and talking at the very top of the Global Library and I instinctively clung to my time regressor disk in fear and guilt, wondering if I should have destroyed the thing along with my self-promised delivery to the front gates of the elusive cosmic creation. I thought I was a devolutionist and operated on linear time, that there was a beginning and end, a sequential game of chess where the order of the mind was God's country. God.

…But Noah took me for a loop. And we had danced in circles as the workers kept the hive tidy with law and cause, keeping infinite potential hidden under the translucent wings of the queen. So how could I know? How could I have known I cast no shadow against the cave walls?

Light everywhere…and uncomfortable warmth. I caught a glimpse of hundreds of mirrors above, situated outside against the sky and inside, to further catch the sun and direct it to various receptive instruments bolted down on the expansive black tiled floor.

With my eyes squinting, I felt Noah take my thin arm and lead me to a designated area where I was given a completely transparent helmet tinted for protection with some black silver synthetic bond. Then, very cautiously, a technician took my invention and respectfully held it for me while several other technicians dressed me in a strange kind of light silvery textured suit and gloves resembling weightless chain mail. Then, making sure none of my surface skin was exposed, the very young-faced man holding my disk spoke to me through his smoky face visor.

"Here you go." He smiled, carefully handing it back to me. "You're going to need that, miss. Never know what life may bring." Then he winked and walked to a different station. At his workbench there was an image of a human heart pumping blood on a small resonance screen and next to the display of this deeply familiar image was another screen with numbers appearing at every cardiac beat along with a wired apparatus leading to a huge gaping dish pointed toward the sky.

Noah appeared before me looking like a silver star voyageur bathed in the soft glow of direct filtered sunlight. He smiled that mischievous smile and slowly put up his gloved hands, flexing them and diagonally placing one across the other, making the universal sign language equivalent of "time-out". He came close so I could hear him and began shouting excitedly.

"It wasn't hard to find you!" he yelled, wide-eyed and almost impatient. "Our solar instrumentation thought it picked up on a stray terrestrial signal, but it turned out to be a human being. Then, we found a direct correlation between your energy emission and the frequency of our strongest extraterrestrial waves and that its light path was re-routing and passing through you along its cyclical transmission trip."

Noah was leading me through the maze of workstations to an elevated platform that emanated a heat I could feel even through my suit. There was a whole team of technicians waiting there and looking at me as if I was some new form of undiscovered species.

"Why?" Noah asked rhetorically. "Why is it channeling its signal through you? Well, it's because of your little tinkering with Father Time. It didn't take us long to discover that in your maverick activities you had harnessed the regulation of the cosmic information flux through some kind of entropy assessment and regression principle.

"During all your skipping backward, you forgot to work yourself into the equation, becoming a sponge of the frequency information contained in the energy around you. You've become a walking receiver of concentrated wave theory and our Alpha signal thinks you're a super-luminous energy-based life form just like itself! Imagine that…!"

I wasn't feeling too well. The physical disintegration was starting again and as I stood, I felt my skin tighten around my bones, my muscles atrophy and my hands and head shake involuntarily. I could have set the coordinates on my disk to gain back one minute, one hour, one day, one life, but the hands would always push forward, and I would laugh, shaking my head to myself, chastising my arrogance.

Yet, the heart is whispering, "forward", and I know I will see Noah again, somewhere beyond the twelfth hour and never before the first can begin. I fell. The absorption of energy was accelerating my growth. I was dying but they picked me up and laid me down on a hard sanitized flatbed. Noah looked down at me.

"We never took your invention, your dream, for property." he whispered. "This was an outside call…" He took my limp hands and cradled them around the disk, holding it before my face. "You are our connection. We don't know how to work the damn thing anyway."

Noah laughed and a tear dropped from his open eyes and fell on the inside of his visor, rolling down leaving a streak.

"We need to know why, we must know, why we are collecting synaptic ghosts…Be our blind ambassador and speak to heaven. Be our light."

"I'm sorry," I whispered, more to humanity that to anyone else. "I'm sorry I took you for granted."

I released the ghost, seeing the stars in the faces around me.

I will not let them fall.

With trembling fingers, I set the coordinates on my invention and time regressed along that Alpha wave of light taking me along with it to the source of that transmitted extraterrestrial signal. My brain shattered into dancing light saturated fractals and although the transmission didn't communicate to me in words, the first mutually understood ideas shared with me was that my heart had stopped but its rhythm had been picked up by the light's particular wave frequencies.

It was an easy transition, from bio-morphic to eternal and at first, I damned the coffin I was in, but quickly realized it had become a lifeboat on which I could ride the waves. It spoke to me about many things, this force, but I did not retain, not having the chains of mortality and the passing of time on my side for memory…Light everywhere and inseparable from who I thought I was. I flew on the ether of the cosmic plasma, an envoy of humanity to bring a message that we had finally encoded a language behind the manifestations of life. We read. We read! We finally read!

The hands frozen on twelve, the sun directly above so my shadow hides within the zero-radius singularity, so no one sees the darkness my movements cast. One signal, one moment of creation, regressing in time to push the baby back in. I am here and now, here and now at the transmitter. I am blinded within the gut of a sun. Jesus! I am here and now, Guardian #126. Blinded.

Instantly, I learn of the brilliant, looped hierarchy effect of the cosmic data bit mind and I re-materialize out of pure potential to be here and now…Now…I am the information. You are the information. Open your eyes to the DNA unity, the principles of the mind's eye manifested as flesh. You are my connection. You are the information…. information…Laughter in the sun. This is our cosmic invitation and I have arrived at the alpha signal…We are born…

Now!

It is a Sunday afternoon in the early summer of 2022. I am trying to fly a plywood airplane, the kind you buy at the counters of hobby shops for a buck and a half. It's flipping and flopping around unsuccessfully in the warm still 86 degrees air and I erroneously persist in making it fly.

It is an average afternoon at the park and in the distance there's a water fountain and a little arch of water perpetually flowing out and down the drain. From far away it looks as if the water is stationary, not moving at all and frozen in time, but on second look, I am mistaken. It is indeed moving through time.

My name is Dr. Edith Wyman and I'm in my early thirties. I'm a mathematician. I make bridges. I make sure their structure is sound, that they maintain their "structural integrity" after years and years of use of getting people from one place to another. People like going places, especially if it involves bridges. Bridges are very important things if where you want to go can't be reached any other way. Don't you think?

A child is crying. I run over to a stroller decorated in sky blue cloth spotted with dancing gray elephants that is parked under a tree. I pick up the baby, looking into the familiar eyes, the child's eyes, *my own eyes*, and see the light buried deep within them. I start swaying the child on my hips back and forth to calm his utter frustration.

"I think it's feeding time." My husband says. He is looking up at me from his seated position under the tree. He searches in a big blue bag for a bottle and gets up so that we are at eye level. He strokes my son's wispy brown hair and then my own.

The sunlight is pouring through the tree leaves, playing off Noah's face, and I feel the afternoon heat warming the back of my neck and shoulders. We are both barefoot and our shoes sit perched up against the tree like an old, retired couple waiting for us to come back for them, waiting there forever.

I think of all the bridges I've built, through all the years and smile while touching the plywood plane's nozzle to my son's own little upturned nose. He gurgles and grasps for the thing. My husband's face, my son's face, their faces carry the light, whispering, "You are blessed. You are the envoy."

Data-Keeper #126 switches places with me and bends down to place my son on his knee to feed him. He looks happy. I am glad.

Ross

"You look tired, dear." My husband Noah sighs. "Maybe we should go soon. I have court tomorrow…"

I take Noah's head in my hands, and we kiss, seeing the crossroads beneath our feet. I open my eyes and he is stroking my face.

"Thank you for being the mother of my child." He confides lovingly.

I see the image of the sun in the sky reflected in his eyes.

"Don't mention it…" I answer.

Afterward we go home and the sun sets. We choose to live in the silence and the darkness. We choose not to acknowledge.

"Welcome, my son," I whisper. "Welcome to your destiny."

"WE ARE THE COSMOS INFORMATION BANK AND WE SHALL PRESERVE THE DATA FLOW IN OUR EVOLUTION…"

Tracy Ross is the author of three collections of poetry and a fictional, dystopia memoir. Her new work, Binary Logic, was inspired by her graduate thesis work on learning science and technology, as well as her work in poetics as part of finishing her MFA at Augsburg University, Minneapolis. She lives and works in Minnesota.

Please visit https://www.rosspoet.org/

www.ingramcontent.com/pod-product-compliance
Lightning Source LLC
Chambersburg PA
CBHW062122020426
42335CB00013B/1057